T5-AQR-250

Bratbusters!

Say Goodbye to Tantrums and Disobedience

Douglas H. Ruben, Ph.D.

Copyright 1992 by Skidmore-Roth Publishing, Inc.

All rights reserved. No part of this book may be copied or transmitted in any form or by any means without written permission of the publisher.

ISBN 0-944132-61-8

Published by Skidmore-Roth Publishing, Inc.
1001 Wall Street
El Paso, Texas 79915
1-800-825-3150   1-915-544-3150

Printed in the United States of America

To Belle and Chuck
The Bratbuster Experts

Introduction

When times are rough, and kids are tough...Who ya gonna call? *Bratbusters!* That's right. That's what you'll become. It's a funny name but it says a mouth full in one word—*Bratbuster!* Busting up old habits, busting up fears, and saying goodbye to bad behavior. Getting rid of them. And knowing exactly how you did it and why it worked. That's what this book is all about.

This book teaches you--the parents, teachers, baby-sitters, grandparents, and even nannies--how to be a Bratbuster using the simple, ready-to-use methods in each chapter. Methods offer rapid ways to stop temper tantrums and noncompliance in less than a month. Nothing hard, nothing to memorize. Just basic principles put into easy terms for dealing with everyday child problems. That is, principles effectively shown to work in 20 plus years of research in the behavioral sciences. Now these technical ideas are distilled down to their barest essentials for your use and enjoyment.

You'll first learn why kids are good and bad. This involves dispelling myths about children and seeing exactly what goes on with behavior. Second, you'll get a picture perfect idea of why kids have tantrums, and then reasons not to take tantrums so personally. Advice follows with precise methods on stopping tantrums and noncompliance. And how about your anger? It can be under control, but it might fly loose at other times. Chapter 6 tells you exactly why you get angry and what to do about it.

Make a special point of reading Chapter 7, "Is there life after children?" It covers what most parenting books never talk about, like raising kids as a single parent, working parent, divorced, and in stepfamilies. And the perennial questions are answered, such as "How do I cool down my child after a visit with my ex-spouse?" The last, on day care, is emotionally relevant to today's dilemma of sending kids to daycare versus keeping them at home. Benefits and risks and why research says what it says will help working parents make prudent decisions.

The last chapter is a guideline for therapy. Just in case what you learn in this book is not enough. *Bratbusters* offers solutions for most types of tantrums, noncompliance, and general misbehavior in children just months old to age 12 and 13. It's basically a book on handling *children*, not older adolescents. But clinically speaking, a little patchwork here and there on the techniques makes them practical for adolescents as well.

Bratbusters does something else for you. It goes beyond just technique. You'll find strategy the easy part. *The really interesting part is knowing why kids behave in certain ways, why you react in certain ways, and formulas to predict why kids and parents react in general.* That's what graduates people from parents to *Bratbusters*, and keeps you there as long as you need the skills, just like riding a bicycle. Once you learn it, you'll never forget it. Never.

Just ask the many *Bratbusters* who were behind this book. Special thanks are owed to key people who inspired pages of this book to fruition. First and foremost are the nearly 2,000 parents, children and families I clinically served over the last 15 years, in outpatient and residential settings. Working with difficult households, happy households, and to-be parents helped to shape methods into practical, ready-to-use form.

I am also grateful to many individuals supportive of this project or participating in different stages of its development. Thanks to Ms. Kim Sweeney, Sitters on Site, for pumping up this fantastic program. To Sheila Ledesma for her insights on cooling down kids after visitations. To Tony Erb for technical assistance. And to Marilyn, my wife, for defending these methods and becoming an expert *Bratbuster*.. Her continued enthusiasm and painstaking typing during my eye injury were spectacular. Just as she is a spectacular mother to Michael and Jennifer.

D.H.R.

Okemos, MI 1991

Table of Contents

Side-effects of too much anger
What control really is
Rewarding exchanges
Punishing exchanges
Simultaneous/delayed exchanges

Married with children
How to make time for yourself and spouse
How to let kids become independent
Working parents
How not to feel guilty
How to balance priorities
How to make your own free time
How to make your spouse help out
Single Parents
How do you play both mom and dad?
How do you introduce your "date" to kids?
Will kids be more masculine or feminine?
Divorced Parents
How to calm down your child after visitation
How do you talk to "ex" about child
problems?
Stepparenting
Problems to watch out for.

Why is day care bad?
Why is day care good?
Why there are no straight answers

Do you feel lonely?
How to beat the lonely trap and find the best
daycare
Choosing the right daycare

Chapter 9.
When is Therapy Needed?

Who says behavior is wrong?
Getting down to basics
When is bad behavior really okay?
When to seek therapy
Behaviors in the danger zone
(Attention-deficit disorder, autism
eating disorders, etc.)
Watch out for labeling your child
Finding a therapist
Shopping for effective therapy
When does therapy work?
When is it time to stop therapy?

CHAPTER 1

Good Kids and Bad Kids

Amy doesn't pay attention to her teacher at school.

Willie fights with other boys.

Joe spray paints obscenities on public property.

Who are these children? Anyone you know? Would you want your child to play with them?

These children come from any lifestyle, from any background. They are any child who does things that people say are "bad." They are "bad" because they have a *problem*. Other people you talk with will agree—"yes, there is something definitely wrong with these children." But why? Why are they so bad? What makes them bad?

Let's consider Amy. She rarely does anything good. Her teacher may feel Amy has a "learning problem." Or, the school counselor may say Amy has a "poor attitude." Her parents hope this badness will disappear as she gets older; that she's just going through a "stage."

Why do they all think this way? Because teachers, counselors and parents learn from many supposed "experts" that children go through stages. Predictable stages. Unavoidable stages. And that their child will grow out of this behavior after the stage passes.

But this is not true. Talking about bad behavior as a stage of growth leads you nowhere. It's tempting to do it but the end result is another myth. Stages of growth are like other myths we all invent to explain why behavior occurs. This whole book puts to rest many myths about raising children and this chapter is a good starting point.

Myths about child rearing must be dispensed with to be *effective* parents. Myths start as advice on handling your child that you get from friends, relatives and trusted others. Many ideas are special and really seem perfect.

Other ideas on what to do and what not to do create more out of a situation than is really needed. For example, take the longstanding advice that showing excessive affection spoils the child. He becomes selfish, unruly, and demands instant gratification. Is this true? Even though hugs and kisses are natural forms of affection, is too much affection no good?

Of course not. Years ago, thinking was that children were spoiled and required from an early age proper self-discipline to remain out of sight and out of mind. The less heard from the better. Children were not the center of family attention and given low priority.

But those days are gone now. Children occupy a central role in the family circle. Unfortunately, the attitude emerging from those days still is believable today by many people.

In this chapter and in the rest of this book, focus shifts from "myths" to what exactly is going on. That is, on the *natural events* of children. Natural events are the real things a child says or does. Five-year old Billy spills milk on his mother's new dress. Is he a "bad" boy? Should he have known better or could he have prevented it? Is he testing his mother by doing this?

Such questions fool parents into thinking their children really are tiny adults conspiring to ruin their world. But not true. Looking at it differently, what really happened? What were the natural events? Here, the natural events included "what was spilled," "who spilled it" and "what to do about it."

Natural events distill very complex action into simple, nonemotional ways of looking at it. It is almost like "turning off" your anger and saying to yourself, "okay, stick only with what Billy did, and not with why he did it." No reading into it. No analyzing it. No probing it's reasons, and no blaming the child. Avoiding the trap of personalizing bad behavior through natural events is shown in Chapters 3 (Never Take It Personally) and 6 (Controlling Your Anger).

The first thing to do, then, is arm yourself against making myths. This chapter helps you do this in two ways. First, learn myths about child-rearing. Second, learn natural ways to look at good and bad behavior.

Myths about Child-Rearing

Myths about child rearing endure even though they are out-dated or do not deal with natural events. Let's consider the following 5 myths and why they must be from removed from everyday life.

The Myths:

1.   *Children go through specific stages of growth.*
2.   *Children inherit their personalities.*
3.   *"Good" children are "smart" and "bad" children are "dumb."*
4.   *Morality is part of being human.*
5.   *It's always the child's fault.*

Myth 1: Children go through specific stages of growth.

It certainly warms the heart to think your child's silly antics will vanish in a year or two. Many people believe this. First it was Sigmund Freud. This trained neurologist took a unique interest in adult neurotic personality and linked it with sexual development. True, sexual development or "maturation" is a normal biological process. The body's structure grows and this coincides with age. The child's feet get bigger, he gets taller, and he develops in genital areas. But the same is not necessarily true for behavior and emotions.

Is there really such thing as "stages of behavioral growth?" Not really. If so, it would mean that all children move through identical phases of emotional and behavioral maturity in the same way as a moth's metamorphosis from cocoon to butterfly. At each stage universal changes would unravel.

For example, all 2-year olds would refuse instructions. All 3-year olds would start talking. Whatever one child did, another child his same age, in the same "stage," also would do. Clone after clone, children would follow identical patterns of progress into adulthood.

Well, so much for fantasy. Children at same ages differ in behavior and this is particularly evident with same age children around the world, living in different countries. Theorists like Freud, Piaget and Kohlberg who proposed "stages of development" realized there was variation. No child did exactly what another child did. Children in France may talk faster than children in England. Children in Russia may crawl or walk earlier than American-born children. And the reasons are self-evident.

Consider, for instance, why children born in Iowa may take longer to develop hand and motor coordination than children born in the Rocky Mountains. The rugged, mountainous terrain puts children through more efforts at walking than would a flat Iowa terrain. Meaning, differences in children rely more on the physical setting as well as social setting during child-rearing years.

"Stage theory" makes another mistake. It assumes kids will *automatically* proceed from one stage to another. Today Johnny mutters "ah, ah." And so his parents predict that in so many months, days and hours, Johnny's vocabulary will enlarge to full words and sentences. Why? Because parents learn that talking—like reading, writing and toilet-training—all surface on their own in time.

Granted, children do speak gradually in more vowels and consonants. Sounds do increase to words and sentences. But this is not automatic. There are very specific experiences needed to occur between child and his world. Language, like toileting and all the rest, is at the mercy of what the child *learns*. What is said and done by parents, family and friends, shapes, or maintains or ruins important skills in the child's life.

Myth 2: Children inherit their personalities.

There are no Surgeon General warnings that parents with bad personalities may endanger personalities of their offspring. But believe it or not, many scientists think personalities are inherited. Studies in the 1960's and 1970's reported that schizophrenic children had schizophrenic parents. Researchers even claimed that offspring twins of schizophrenic parents, reared apart, still showed clues of schizophrenia. Similar claims always are heard about alcoholic families, that children of alcoholics inherit genes predisposing them to become drinkers.

Take a young girl named Katie. Katie yells and screams at her friends. Her parents also are screamers. Does this make Katie a screamer due to inheritance? Genes do transfer from parent to child in many known ways.

Usually heredity plays a role in hypertension, diabetes, blindness, blood diseases and congenital physical disabilities. This genetic grapevine puts a child at biological risk. So, is the same true for a psychological risk? In honesty, no, there is no definite genetic linkage that puts children absolutely at psychological risk.

So, why do children behave much like their parents? The answer again falls back on learning. A personality consists of chunks of behavior. Verbal and nonverbal behavior; this means how a parent talks, acts, reacts, and handles daily life. Children watching this behavior are prime imitators of their parents, duplicating every step of action absorbed in their observation. If Jerry is hot-tempered, impulsive, and nasty to people, chances are that somebody treated him that way during early formative years when Jerry was impressionable. Blaming Jerry's acting out on heredity, on his family's ancestry of tyranny, misses the point entirely. It overlooks specific influences in his life causing that behavior.

As for the term "personality," it really is too obscure to mean anything. A personality is a class of behavior rather than some abstract human fiber located near the tibia. Nobody ever *saw a personality*. What we see in children is their actions, their words, and how they interact with people. Seen are natural events.

Myth 3: Good children are smart and bad children are dumb.

It's tough enough raising a child everyone says is "slow." But when parents start labeling their own children, problems really explode.

This happened to Amy. Amy didn't do good behavior. In fact, she was a nuisance in school. She ignored instructions, distracted other students, stood up from her chair, and never paid attention to lesson plans. Amy then went for psychological testing and was diagnosed as a slow learner with low intelligence.

Amy, and kids like her, receive labels like "slow learner," "learning impaired," "emotionally impaired," "learning disabled," and "developmentally disabled" based on the best intentions of people to help them through life. Labels get stamped onto children who do things that parents, teachers, and adults in general dislike and think is deviant. Children who behave worse than average or are believed to be "slow" get labelled for it. But labels also convey the attitude that low intelligence *means* bad behavior.

This is a myth because "intelligence" strays from natural events. Intelligence itself poses a unique problem. No one has ever seen intelligence where scientists say intelligence should be—in the brain. Intelligence doesn't exist in there. In fact, it doesn't exist anywhere. That is, anywhere like a physical organ might exist. People just think intelligence belongs in the brain since thinking and other human functions originate from there.

But intelligence *per se* is neither a physical organ nor is it a basic human function. Heart, lungs, liver, pancreas, stomach, intestines—all of these are actual physical organs located beneath the skin. Walking, talking, breathing and eating are all basic human functions. We can see, touch, smell and taste them. But never with intelligence. Intelligence is an elusive, abstract function created in people's minds as a warehouse for the strange features that separate man from animal. Memory, thoughts, imagination—all of these "special" traits supposedly need a "special" storage tank. And intelligence is created as that storage tank.

So what is it, then, that psychological tests measure and everybody bases their decisions on for labeling children? Learned behaviors. Tests measure a sample of verbal and motor behaviors the a child learns up to a point in his life. Lack of learning or having poor skills means the child performs below standards, below the average. Strong learning ability or having strong skills means the child performs above or at the average. This is all people are talking about regarding intelligence. Nothing more than that.

So when a child labelled as bad also scores poorly on an intelligence test, rather than jump to conclusions about how bad he is, ask instead why *the child's behavior is a problem, what causes that problem, and what can be done about it.* This approaches more logically the range of natural events involved.

Myth 4: Morality is part of being human.

Janice returned home one day after Sunday school. She overheard her mother talking on the telephone with her Sunday school teacher. The word "morality" came up. Janice looked puzzled.

And so should we. Morality is a strange word. It tries to encompass so much about human duty, religion, and social obligation that it usually goes beyond natural events. Morality also creates the myth that children grow up into "moral" persons. True, kids mature biologically. Kids also progress in language from morphenes to phonemes and finally to full sentences. But, like intelligence, natural maturity does not include morality.

Hardly anybody believes morality is genetic. Instead, clergy and most parents believe that morals are part of human experience. Things kids say or do ultimately lead them into situations of *moral consequence.* Michael, for example, stumbled into a moral situation when he stole Brad's bubble gum. The moral? Stealing is bad. This has a Bible-story lesson, where the hero discovers that "fate" caused his downfall. Michael's downfall was getting caught, suffering the punishment, and realizing his act of dishonesty.

On this level morality develops along the lines of most skills through natural experience. But morality taken out of context can be a problem. This is what happens when morality becomes another word for "personality." Mass killers or "psychopaths" are said to be "amoral" (without morals) or "immoral" (against morals). Is it something they lack inside of them? Saying a child is immoral conjures up images of a person with weak or underdeveloped morality much like he has weak or underdeveloped muscles. Supposedly moral children are good children and immoral children are bad children.

The problem here is blaming the child for poor morals. Fault does not lie with children but with the adults failing to teach lessons of right and wrong that establish moral *rules*. Rules, like instructions, start as adult statements of what children should do or should not do, followed by consequences for compliance or noncompliance. Told that if Bobby eats the cookie, he will lose television privileges, Bobby decides not to eat the cookie. Bobby is reacting to rules that guide his behavior under limitations. This is realistically how morality develops.

Myth 5: It's always the child's fault.

Parents regard "good" and "bad" behavior as something *in the child*. Poor cooperation, to them, means the child is bad. He doesn't listen. He doesn't follow directions. He is the one to blame—nobody else. Children get blamed for saying "No!" because of the myth that children cause their own behavior. What Harold says and does is Harold's responsibility. He should know better. Harold leaves his toys on the floor. He refuses to turn off the television. He shrieks loudly calling for mommy when she is on the telephone. Doesn't he know better? Why does he do this?

Anger swells inside of you as you insist that Harold knows better, that he only is testing your limits, and that nobody but Harold is responsible.

There is a problem with this thinking. Blaming Harold overlooks a basic fact of child development. Harold is like any child who does things as a normal part of growing up. Growing up involves interactions with people, objects, events, and exploring the world of attention. Harold also learns from what others say and do to him. In most cases Harold simply reacts to people and changes around him. Yelling at Harold gives him attention and feeds his persistent energy to gain more attention.

Quietly coping with Harold or even ignoring his attention-seeking efforts does the opposite; his annoyances subside. Realizing this, parents must conclude that children between the ages of 1 and 6 have good and bad behavior based on how parents treat them.

This leads to the next section on what type of parental reactions can foster good behavior and what reactions seriously jeopardize a child's mental health.

Natural Ways to Look at Good and Bad Behavior

Put on your new objective eye glasses to figure out if behavior is good or bad. Already it pays off to avoid myths about intelligence, morality, and stages of growth. Surely more myths may arise whenever the natural reasons for action are absent. So, let's stay closely with the facts of parent-child interactions and discover the intriguing relationship that punishment and reward have with behavior outcomes. Oddly, few people ever consider "rewards and punishment" this way. But did you know that too much punishment, presented in certain ways, really can cause strange reactions?

Is there a link between too much adult punishment and childhood problems? Researchers Holmes and Robins most recently verified this longstanding belief by showing that harsh discipline may drive children to alcoholism, depression or some other psychological disturbance in teenage and adult years. Their study joins a collection of research assembled over many years pointing out the same results. Namely, that harsh or unfair discipline in childhood rather than genes may be at the root of emotional problems.

Let's take a closer look at this. As adults, ask yourself whether you currently experience the following difficulties.

1. Do you have trouble expressing feelings?
2. Is it hard for you to relax?
3. Are you loyal beyond reason to any person or cause?
4. Are you overly responsible?
5. Do you fear losing control in situations or over people?
6. Do you have difficulty with personal or even professional relationships?
7. Are you overly self-critical?
8. Are you afraid of being abandoned in re lationships?

An answer of "yes" to at least six of these questions signals an insecurity perhaps not disrupting your life or even job but it lurks inside of you and is linked to your discipline as a child. Strict discipline in your childhood makes you afraid as adults of many things other people accept without problem. Are you afraid you might:

Make an error?
Cause somebody grief?
Embarrass somebody?

> Look stupid?
> Lose control?

Panic rises whenever adults are so self-critical and fearful of being hated that any tiny mistake becomes a catastrophe. How did this attitude start? Was it always there in adulthood or does adult fear feed off of childhood fear? If childhood fears are the source, what instills this fear?

Emotionally angry parents who try to control their children by strict discipline and heavy use of punishment can instill the fear. Ask yourself if your parents' anger was:

1. *Random and arbitrary.* This means it happened inconsistently, without forewarning, and for reasons unknown to you. You may not even have been at fault.

2. *Unavoidable.* This means there was no way to head it off at the pass. Once signs of anger ignited, the chance of preventing or delaying it was impossible.

3. *Inescapable.* This means your attempts to escape from yelling, screaming or punitive discipline

were unsuccessful and impossible. Instead you surrendered to defeat with or without a struggle. Struggling only intensified problems and caused worse wrath and furry. Silence painfully hurt inside and lowered your opinion of yourself but at least it shortened the angry episodes. Sometimes silence escalated your parent's anger, which really confused you on how to react.

4.　*Aggressive.* This means punishment took an outwardly negative form as verbal and physical abuse. Physical abuse included hitting, pushing, slapping, holding, washing your mouth out with soap and use of restraints. Verbal abuse involved constant criticism, insults, and attacks on character.

Anger taken out in these ways can scare children into believing they are inferior, worthless, and constantly under attacks. Other parenting errors usually causing the same outcome and perhaps in your childhood include:

5.　*Absence of affection.* Recall early we made mention of indulgent affection, saying it was perfectly normal. Many families leave it out completely for many reasons, in part because they do not want to spoil the kids. But also because they believe it simply is "wrong." That means no hugging, no kissing, no touching, no tickling, no nothing. Absolutely zero affection takes place in any way, shape or form with the children.

6.   *Absence of opportunities to learn.* This means parents are so busy, so angry, so impatient that they forget to let their kids try out new things. They get frustrated and tie the 2-year old's shoe laces instead of having her try it. They force the clothes on a child instead of letting a child practice this skill for himself. Even little things such as a son turning off his own bedroom light or pouring his own cereal are denied. Parents do it all. And then, later, when feeling overwhelmed, these same parents complain they have lazy children who act like babies.

7.   *Rewards for delay or wrong behavior.* Delay behavior is when normal children get distracted or begin some behavior that postpones what parents asked them to do. It takes all forms. Here are some of them:

a.   arguing and debating with parents

b.   ignoring the parent

c.   tantrums

d.   sustaining interest in an
      activity or task.

Four year old Cheryl, for instance, just continued watching her television show when asked to
move her shoes. Sam, her 3-year old brother, re-
acted to instructions with a tantrum. Sue Ellen, the
oldest at 6 years old, argued with her mother that it
was Cheryl and Sam's job to wash the dishes. Each
child did delay behavior by gaining extra minutes
before being forced into the instructed task.

Parents alert to this trap of delay behavior
can overcome the mistake of making it worse. But
most parents perceive delay behavior as direct defiance of their authority and will react to it nega-
tively. This negative attention acts like a "reward"
because it fuels bad behavior and propels a repeat
performance of delay behavior in the future.

What if the reward is good attention for behavior? Does that work? As this book explores, rewards used correctly pay great dividends in terms of
compliant child behavior. But even hugs, kisses
and sweet words are deadly if given for the wrong
behavior.

For example, take Daryl's sly behavior. He hid from sight so his younger brother could not see him. Then he sprang out like a cat and terrified his brother Terry who cried frantically. Down the stairs their mother ran—desperate to see what had happened. What she found was Daryl comforting his brother Terry with a warm embrace. She praised Daryl for "looking out for his brother."

Is there something wrong with this? Do you get the slight impression that Daryl "did not deserve" praise; that instead, the reward might actually develop *wrong* behavior in the form of sibling antagonism? You're right; this commonly is the result of rewards for wrong behavior.

What toll do parenting mistakes #1 through 7 have on a child? Earlier you checked to see if you experience in your adulthood had any common links to harsh discipline during childhood. An easier way of categorizing childhood reactions is into three groups. These groups represent common warning signs that your child suffers from too much punishment or an uneven balance of reward and punishment. Groups are divided into (a) *behavior excesses*, (b) *behavior deficits*, and (c) *avoidance behavior*.

Behavior Excesses

A behavior excess is when your child reacts in ways beyond the norm for his age group. Defined criteria for this pattern usually include:

1.   Behavior is rapid.
2.   Behavior takes much effort to complete.
3.   Your child demands much feedback on his behavior.
4.   Behavior repels people's attention after a while.
5.   Your child is preoccupied with that behavior or talks much about it.
6.   Your child is aggressive if your feedback on his behavior is delayed.
7.   Your child is noncompliant or argues a lot.

Behavior Deficits

A behavior deficit means his actions fall below standard levels or that he lacks important skills for dealing with demands of the age group. Specifically look to see if:

1.   Behavior is slow.
2.   Behavior takes much effort to complete.

3.   Your child wants little or no feedback on the behavior.

4.   Your child has difficulties relating to his behavior.

5.   Behavior attracts sympathy in other people or people do the behavior for him.

6.   Your child is easily agitated if confronted with the deficiency.

7.   Your child is easily distracted, diverted or procrastinates (seems lazy).

8.   Your child will avoid or escape situations where he must do the deficient behavior.

Avoidant Behaviors

Avoidant behavior, under most circumstances, means your child is afraid. He anticipates criticism, rejection, failure or any punishment so regularly or is so self-critical that attempts at any behavior pose monumental hazards. Look for these warning signs:

1.   Your child is scared to behave in general around other people.

2.   Your child is very selective about his words and actions.

3.   Your child reacts slowly, in small
       amounts or has difficulty with behavior.
4.   Your child delays reacting or wishes to be
       excused quickly when pressed
       to respond in certain ways.
5.   Your child cries easily or is highly
       intimidated.
6.   Your child feigns illness or has frequent
       stomach aches and headaches.
7.   Your child refuses to try new behavior or be
       creative.
8.   Your child sneaks around or does the
       requested behavior when others are gone.

Recognizing these warning signs is the first step to being a *Bratbuster*. It means you are right on target with things going on in your family and ready to press the start button to change bad habits into good habits. A mistake is thinking that you've "ruined" your kids and now they must all undergo counseling, including yourself, before things get worse. Slow down, take a breath. Nobody gets parenting right the first time—not even the second time. Perfection is nice but unrealistic. Instead give yourself a pat on the back for realizing now what you never knew before and for being the first on the block to make changes.

Go through with the steps outlined in this book for yourself and for your children. This will be one less mistake your children will make as parents with kids of their own.

CHAPTER 2

Why Kids Have Tantrums

Yesterday was the straw that broke the camel's back. Just as you stepped out of the shower stretching for the towel, Jordan met your hands halfway. He took the towel from you. Wet, cold and short of patience, you politely asked him to surrender the towel. It didn't work. Again you asked him in a firm voice, some octaves higher. He ignored you and started laughing.

He laughed louder.
You threatened him louder.
He yelled back at you.
You became very angry.
He called you names.
You lost it.

And guess what happened? You gave in to his *tantrum*. Moments earlier you were enjoying a private shower away from the household turbulence. But it was short lived. Jordan's interruption turned personal tranquility into an insane asylum. And tantrums will do that and more if children receive attention for acting out in strange ways.

This chapter gives you the straight scoop on why kids have tantrums, what exactly they are, and personal mistakes parents make trying to out–smart or undermine temper tantrums. Later, in Chapter 4, simple steps are offered to combat angry tantrums. So, let's start with why these things happen in the first place.

Why Do Kids Have Tantrums?

Angry children ages 1 to 3 rarely if ever express the reasons for having temper tantrums. In fact, verbal ability or "expressive language" develops into real communication by the late 3's and into ages 4 and 5. Older children ages 5 and on probably can verbalize reasons but not with the sophistication of adults. So, to the inquiry, "Why did you do that?", very few children have the verbal architecture to reply. They may not even realize their behaviors were "wrong," "offensive" or a tantrum. In fact, many kids consider aggressively acting out a normal reaction to situations.

How, then, do parents really know why kids have tantrums? Unfortunately the common way is by guessing. Chapter 3 explores in depth why guessing backfires because of the wrong inferences made about child behavior. In the meantime, consider the natural events behind a temper tantrum. Children of all ages usually yell, scream or display displeasure leading to anger for 5 reasons:

1. *They are disrupted during a fun or rewarding activity.*
2. *They are punished for wrong behavior.*
3. *They are denied rewarding objects or activities*
4. *They are tired, hungry, sick, or suffering bi ological upset.*
5. *They receive attention for it or get bad things removed.*

They are disrupted during a fun or rewarding activity

This means interrupting your son or daughter while they are watching television or involved in play. Upon interruption they get angry and poorly adjust to the diversion. This is because children basically operate on immediate gratification. Items, things and objects wanted when they want them only becomes a problem when these things are jeopardized. Even if the disruption is momentary—"you can return to it in just a minute"—it doesn't matter. Seconds feel like hours as the child experiences emotional withdrawal from the intoxicating joy of personal toys.

They are punished for wrong behavior

Discipline takes many forms. Simply stating that behavior is inappropriate or that it is *wrong* does more than correct future action. It also stops wrong behavior from continuing at that moment. Your reprimand puts an immediate restraint on acting out that disrupts the behavior and whatever fun kept it alive. Telling Bruce, "enough is enough, cut it out!" terminates his teasing behavior. Removed, also is the laughter kids around him were doing in response to the behavior. Like disrupting a rewarding activity, removal of gratifiers with a rebuke instantly ignites liquid tantrums burning in all directions.

They are denied rewarding objects or activities

Denied means prevented. Children prevented from playing because of bad behavior or other commitments (e.g., "it's dinner time") are angry for this schedule readjustment. Just as children react to immediate gratification, so it is that immediate gratifiers are on a clock–work schedule. Learning is very cyclical at early ages where the order of activities depends on doing it the same way each day. For example, children "know" that after daycare they get a snack, followed by watching Batman on television, followed by dinner. Changes, disruption, interruption or denial of this expected schedule puts them in orbit.

Denial also delays immediate gratification. Your child plans on playing outside but you stop him before he reaches the door. There you explain that dinner tonight is special because mommy and daddy ordered pizza and it arrived just now. But ask yourself. Does he really care? Realize what you have done. You've eliminated highly rewarding fun for him to eat a pizza. Chances are that no matter how good the pizza tastes, your son feels deprived of playtime and will protest this decision.

They are tired, hungry, sick, or suffering biological upset

Let's not forget the obvious. Agitation frequently surfaces from fatigue, or hunger or if your child is ill. Many "biological" causes explain the cranky, disobedient yelling and screaming that has little to do with parental attention or removal of rewards. Commonly these "biological" reasons never start tantrums but act as potent fuel propelling it once rewards are removed or reprimands are given. A sick child, in particular, may be disoriented, weak, and hypersensitive to body ailments that distract him from listening to your words.

They receive attention for it or get bad things removed

The accidental trigger finger is to fight tantrums with resentment and bitter anger. Parents naturally are upset by tantrums and feel they are owed better respect than being terrorized by Godzilla's look–a–like. Anger expressed in a raised voice startles the screaming child only for a moment, until tantrums then intensify. This is of course unacceptable and parents amplify vocal tone feeling that "louder voices will paralyze his actions." The louder it gets, the more attention parents literally are giving to a tantruming child. Just the same is true when parents figure out another strategy. "Ah, if I soften his situation then maybe he'll stop crying." Softening a situation is picking up toys for him or telling siblings or other children to leave him alone. In other words, relieving him of *what you think is making him angry in the first place.*

The danger with caretaking of this sort is that it teaches children the wrong message. That screaming, crying, name–calling and all sorts of nasty tantrums *earns* somebody doing something for you. The impatient 3 year old shouting for somebody to help her tie her shoes has learned that enough screaming spells relief—M–O–T–H–E–R. Mother dear comes to the rescue and thereby stops the crying. Children depending on others to handle their grief get very annoyed, very quickly, when that rescuer is late, unavailable or dares to say, "No, you tie it yourself!"

What Exactly are Tantrums?

There's only one way to describe tantrums: *Frantic fury of fire burning across the sea and threatening all life as far as man can see.* Well, not exactly. Tantrums brew for reasons explained a moment ago and reach different stages depending on attention given to the child. Parts of tantrums really obvious to any parent are *anger, persistence, and rebellion.* Let's look at each one closely.

Anger

Angry children between several months old and 2 years old act on impulse and may say very little about being angry. Reactions are rapid, swift, and involve "gross motor movements." Meaning, they may fall down, bang against things, approach or even destroy property or try annoying the parents. Crying also is part of anger. Lacking much speech, young children resort to grunts, crying, touching and forceful action in hopes of alerting your attention.

Is he really angry? Did I really do something to upset him? Sure, he's angry and plenty frustrated. But not for reasons usually attributed to adult reasons for anger. Your angry, crying child has been deprived of something highly desirable and this makes him upset. Thinking you, personally, are at fault for his anger is wrong.

Persistence

Waiting out a tantrum, also called "ignoring" is one strategy if done correctly. But parents frequently complain that ignoring backfires because unattended children blow a fuse ten times worse than before ignoring them. You can call this behavior "persistence" by its constant momentum. "He keeps yelling and yelling and doesn't shut up. Persistent little bugger, isn't he?" He is persistent, all right, but for another reason.

Attention given on a continuous basis during the tantrum will teach your child to keep the water flowing. Tantrums persist by the child believing that he *will* get what he wants with enough effort expended. When small fits escalate into Mount. St. Helen volcanic eruptions the endurance of a child's efforts correspond to repeated attempts by parents to silence him. The more tries made at inhibiting behavior, the longer behavior stays. The less attention paid to behavior, the shorter the length.

Rebellion

Older children ages 5 to 14 have mature language and use it during an outburst. Words take on explosive meaning that replace the gross motor movements, touching of parent or property destruction. Words also take two varieties. Either they directly insult parents or are debating and accusatory. Insults range from obscenity to repeating words spoken between mommy and daddy or even what mommy and daddy say to the child.

Children learn words have magical powers. They imitate those words out of curiosity. Deliberately using profanity because it is a "wrong word" is done only by angry teens, rarely by younger speaking children. Obscene or nasty words said by a youngster is more "experimenting with language." Trying out funny or big words mom and dad use when they are angry.

Words voicing disagreement are more deceptive. Angry Richard argues that his mother is wrong, that really his brother started the problem, and that everybody hates him. Is he really rebellious? Are these words intentionally opposing parental rules? Again, children are not adults; they do not think like adults. They do not act like adults. And they do not have experience like adults. Just because children argue does not mean they *challenge the rules*. It means they are looking to buy time or delay doing the activity or behavior change requested of them. Arguments postpone, until later, an assigned task or chore.

Arguments also hide the child's own vulnerability. Angry Richard hates being criticized. The older and more talkative he is, the more he tries combating people who yell and scream at him. Anytime he made errors in the past mom or dad got on his case. Now he tries hard to counter their critical attacks with insults, accusations and profanity that is so shocking that it stops the criticism. His parents are dumbfounded by his attacks and respond aggressively. You might think—has Richard really gained anything by his nasty behavior? His parents are still mean. True, but they no longer for the moment are critical about the error he made. Richard escaped the criticism with a diversion called "tantrums."

Personal Mistakes with Tantrums

Many high-rising anxieties from temper tantrums are because parents work too hard to eliminate them. Needs to censor the behavior immediately vary with all situations. Yelling in church is embarrassing and a parent may quickly silence his child. In grocery stores yelling is more tolerable but still a nuisance and draws attention from nosy customers. Again, rapid censorship results.

Censorship takes many forms and few if any of the traditional methods do the trick. Here are a list of common mistakes in handling temper tantrums and why they fail:

1. Yelling and shouting
2. Physical punishment
3. Bribing silence
4. Threats, dirty looks, and snapping fingers
5. Insults
6. Talking it out
7. Time out
8. Sending to the bedroom
9. Going without dinner (any meal)
10. Removal of privileges
11. Grounding

Yelling and Shouting.

Forget it. This is an adult temper tantrum. Frustration no doubt doubles in size but when parents raise voices they are inviting the children to copy this behavior. Whether or not tantrums momentarily stop, ultimately children see that "this is the way to get something you want—by yelling."

Physical Punishment

Again, this form of discipline instructs children on how to do it to somebody else from whom they want instant obedience (e.g., dogs, cats, baby brother, sister, etc.). Physical punishment also induces fear into children unnecessarily. Yes, it interrupts tantrums and may even stop them, but for the wrong reason: The child is stung by surprise, intense fear and shock. Effects of this shock also are short–lived. As a rule, effects of punishment rarely if ever endure on human behavior.

A third drawback is that punished anger finds another outlet for expression. Children stifled by a spanking, the strap or some instrument may withdraw in tears. Later that day or evening don't be surprise if he tears up his room or stuffs toilet paper down the toilet, or ruins his personal property. Is this an act of frustration or retaliation? Not *retaliation* like adults do it. Retribution for a child is different from retribution by the KKK. The child is not aiming to get back at you but instead *needs* to express hurt, fear and anger and unfortunately does so in destructive ways. He would just as much tear apart his own socks as he would your pair of socks. *Whose socks they are, is irrelevant.*   Punishment forces him into alternative ways to be angry.

Bribing Silence

"Please keep quiet...pretty please...with gum drops on top?" Glorified promises and rewards for silence get into a mess if done incorrectly. Parents make the mistake of offering the reward *during* the outburst and this teaches the child to stop his behavior for the reward. So, did it work? No, it didn't work. Offering rewards while tantrums are in mid–stride actually teaches children to repeat the tantrum knowing rewards will be available. Rewards instead should be given for good behavior, not for terminating bad behavior.

Threats, Dirty Looks and Snapping Fingers

If looks could kill, many parents would be in jail. Eye glances, facial expressions of disapproval and finger snapping make up the finer art of adult nonverbal behavior. When too many people are around, nonverbal cues disguise parental anger and still get the message across. Children reacting to these abstract cues are in for a big surprise when they grow up and interact with the rest of child and adult world. Anytime people show these or similar facial expressions your child will *instantly* assume the worst. "My goodness! What did I do wrong?"

The danger with relying on facial expressions, gestures and nonverbal cues is that they are confusing and look too much like what other people say or do when not angry.

Threats are another issue. Threats typically state a serious consequence will follow if tantrums continue. So, what happens is the child continues to misbehave until that awful consequence begins? Many times that awful consequence never occurs or parents forget to do it. Hollow threats quickly teach kids not to take seriously what parents have to say. Since threats are another form of "instructions," ignored threats may mean instructions get the cold shoulder as well.

Insults

Lowering your child's esteem with an insult is a back–handed way to calm behavior. Some parents believe one terrific blow to confidence will force the child to be aware of his mistake. This is along the same lines as shaking a person until he awakes to consciousness. Of course there are many problems with this approach. First, insults will emotionally scare a child already struggling with low self–esteem. Second, insults do little to actually change tantrums and the child learns absolutely nothing beneficial from them. What he *does* learn is to feel like dirt, be like dirt and think of himself or herself as dirt. One child was called "Little Jerk" so much during infancy that by the time he started kindergarten he actually thought his name was "Little Jerk."

Talking It Out

Today's parents are up on new and caring approaches to child raising. Many books, articles and talk shows say that loving parent–child relationships begin when parents explore reasons for child misbehavior. "Ask your child why he is feeling upset with you and what can be done about it." Sadly, children below age 4 who are asked these questions will only interpret the question as attention for behavior. Nothing more. They do not think in abstract concepts such as "dealing with feelings" and "resolution." Problem–solving during tantrums is inadvisable largely because it fuels behavior and makes arguments between parent and child worse. Talking it out after the tantrum is over, and with a speaking child, is the better alternative.

Time Out

Parents who read or stay on top of educational methods of child discipline no doubt are familiar with the legendary "time–out." Time–out has an interesting history in research with all sorts of children with all sorts of behavior problems. It can be highly effective. But time–out for tantrums is not appropriate. A time–out is when you interrupt the misbehavior and ask him to sit, stand, lay or go to another part of the house. Frequently it is to sit in a chair. Children sit for different lengths of time ranging from 5 minutes to 1 hour. How long should they sit there? That all depends on the behavior and procedure of time–out, which unfortunately goes beyond the scope of this chapter.

Why time–out is a no–no for tantrums is that it provides volumes of attention for the angry, crying child. Interrupting him in the middle of a fit to relocate his body in a chair forces you to have verbal and physical contact with him. Any contact is harmful during tantrums. Even if he goes to the time–out chair, does he stay there? On top of tantruming, he now is getting up from the chair. Your rage intensifies by his double disobedience. Instead, don't use time out and stay away from giving unnecessary instructions when tantrums are in heat.

Sending To the Bedroom

"Get out of my sight and into your bedroom, you miserable brat." Sound familiar? Anger tends to bring out the best in adults and sending a child to his bedroom ranks as the most popular method of tantrum control. Although, unfortunately, there is very little control exerted from it. Ordering his evacuation from the room may relieve the angry parent and possibly restore peace and quiet to on-lookers. But what does it really do? A child who leaves the scene of the crime (tantrum) *never learns what to do differently in the angry situation. He does learn how to escape an angry situation by having a tantrum.* Sending the child to his room relieves him of his anger, his bad behavior and basically can be quite a reward. Instead, keep him in the ugly situation where he can learn constructive alternatives.

Going Without Dinner (any meal)

Upset parents tend to deny a meal to angry children because they feel they "deserved it." Perhaps this is what their parents did to them or they honestly believe that removal of meals will *force him to think about his bad actions.* Once again, young children will not "think about their bad actions" like adults do. A child sent to bed without his dinner will not sit on his bed contemplating the morality of his action. Never. He might cry, be upset, play with local toys, or simply fall asleep. Then, he will likely awake in the middle of the evening starving to death.

Removal of Privileges

Bad actions lose privileges. Privileges from watching television to playing outdoors are dangled like a carrot over the child's head for good or bad behavior. The correct use of privileges can make bad behavior go away very effectively. But not with tantrums. Yelling, screaming, pounding and verbal abuse from a child is magnified in living color when parents inform him he lost his privileges. Reasons are obvious. First, telling him about this loss acts as attention for the tantruming behavior. Second, removal of rewards always provokes more anger, besides the shock waves already in motion. Third, removal of anything on a frequent basis teaches children to want little, play with few things, and basically disown property because it no longer has a lasting rewarding value.

Grounding

The last common approach to tantrums is to ground the child. Keep him home or away from desired activities for a day, two days, one week or even a month on account of his rude behavior. It doesn't work for tantrums. Tantrums are attention–seeking actions or actions to delay, prevent or get out of bad situations. By grounding a child, you accidentally permit him the outcome he wanted from the tantrums of avoiding or escaping situations. Little if any constructive learning is accomplished from the discipline.

All in all, even the best intentioned parents may use strategies leading to more and more tantrums. Kind–hearted and emotional love accidentally spills over in the form of exploring, probing and discovery of tantrums which worsens them. Then, too, anger, frustration, or simply outright physical punishment shocks children into fear and doubt. What remains, then? Chapters 4 and 5 introduce a step–wise approach, tested and used so widely across the nation and by millions of parents, that it really has the Midas touch you're looking for.

CHAPTER 3

Never Take It Personally

You're losing control and all you can think about is "why me?" He's trapping me again. He's pushing my buttons. He's testing me to the limits. Now he knows my weak spots and is ahead of the game. He's in control and I'm his slave. No mercy. He's winning and I'm losing.

This scenario of thinking is very common among parents who believe their children are up to no good. Believing this implies that things kids say and do have a deeper meaning. Beneath the surface of action they must have other intentions, like adults do, for being so rotten, so often. The idea that misbehavior is a front for a hidden agenda brings us to the point of this chapter: That adults slip and slide through the muddied waters of assumptions.

They read very deeply into action and make more out of events than probably is necessary. "Mommy, I hate you!" hurts because it is taken personally. Parents read between the lines, between the words, and are suspicious of motivations of children.

Taking behavior so personally does not start once adults become parents. Usually these are sensitive adults who have lifelong tendencies to over react to situations or they may constantly worry what others think of them. Fear of rejection, of failure, of lacking control—all of these raise a parent's antennae to pick up wavelengths about anything and everything around them. This particularly is strong around kids who they sincerely believe are angry at them.

A closer look at assumptions and why parents take things so personally involves three topics. The first is getting a precise idea of what assumptions consist of and how easy they are to make. Second is realizing that so much of personalizing hedges on values or "beliefs." Some beliefs are perfectly honorable whereas other beliefs, called "irrational beliefs," push beyond healthy ways of perceiving the child's situation. Third, accept the ways to prevent and overcome traps of assumptions.

What do Assumptions Consist of?

Think about that word *assumptions* for a moment. What does it mean? Few people actually ponder over definitions of a word but this is a word worth considering. To "assume," means guessing information about some situation because relevant facts are missing. Sam wakes up early on Saturday morning, disrupting the whole household. Awakened by his playful noises, what goes through your mind?

•That he is disruptive?

•That he knows better than to disturb us?

•That he has no respect and is rude?

•That he must be taught a lesson so this never happens again?

"Yes" to any one of these puts you in line for making assumptions. Now ask how many actual facts you knew about Sam's behavior.

•Do you know why—I mean, really *know why* Sam is up?

•Do you know what he is doing?

•Do you have all the facts regarding his behavior?

Generally the answer to these questions is "no." Unless directly in sight of his behavior, facts about what he is doing and why are absent or fuzzy.

When facts are lost and you feel that urgent need to figure out his behavior, here's what happens:

You Take A Guess!

That's right. Good old fashion guesswork shifts into gear. Piece by piece you splice together the motives, reasons and action as if solving a crossword puzzle. Answers to the mystery unravel with probing, prodding and relying on intuition. But that's exactly where problems first arise. All guesswork is plagued by reading into behavior in these three ways:

1.   *Guessing based on what he's done in the past.*
2.   *Guessing based on why you would do it (your motives).*
3.   *Guessing based on certain beliefs about things and people.*

Guessing based on what he's done in the past.

First thought upon hearing Sam's loud noises is "well, whenever he's done that in the past it's been because. . . therefore that must be why he's doing it now." Reasons that explained his behavior yesterday, the day before, perhaps even a month ago, automatically serve as the main course on why he *must* be doing it now. In fact, no other explanation crosses your mind.

How this occurs is interesting. Most adults think very rapidly and in abbreviations. That is, few people really go through the tedious labor of saying to themselves, "gee whiz, in the past when he has done this it was for this reason, therefore doing the same behavior today must mean it is for the same reason." Hardly any adult thinks this way. Instead, quick thinking makes these phrases go rapidly and all you consciously hear yourself thinking is something like, "there he goes again. . ." or "he's starting it now. . ." or possibly, "oh, no, not again." As if to say, "oh, no, not again *that he'll wake up everybody in the household.* " The latter part is unnecessary and rarely heard. Brief indented phrases carry the full message about why you believe Sam is up to no good.

Guessing based on why you would do it (your motives).

Another easy way to figure out behavior is looking inward to yourself. Ask yourself, "okay, why would I do such and such?" Self–motives deal less with your past as a child than with your adult reasons. As an adult, "Why would I do such and such? Why would I awake early in the morning like Sam does? "Ah, it's because he's worried about something." Here the appointed reason pertains to *why you would do the same behavior as an adult.*

Guessing based on certain beliefs about things and people.

All of us form views about the world. Some views are flexible, others inflexible. Flexible views perceive the world as things that you would like to see happen but may not happen. It's not a catastrophe if life does not work out the way you hope it will. Then again, values dictating that life must follow a rigid order and for every behavior there is a reason, may put you in the dog house. Inflexible views or "beliefs" generate absolutes about how life must and should be and they usually take two forms. First is regarding other people. Second is regarding yourself.

Other People. How easy it is to say "he should have done this," or "Sam never does this right." Blaming your child for imperfection means not having any tolerance for his mistakes. Errors he makes inconvenience your life and cause unwanted changes in schedule. Parents caught in this trap tend to blame children for everything.

Yourself. Other parents dare not blame other people because they, themselves, are at fault. Self–indictment means imposing the same intolerance to mistakes in yourself. "I should have done this," or "I never do this right." These comments indulge in self–criticism, stretching your expectations for perfection way beyond possibility. You leave no margin for error; everything done incorrectly or inadequately toward the children becomes a sin, a vice and deepens your guilt.

Looking at these guesses again, notice that all three rush together to form assumptions. Again, they include:

1.   Guessing based on what he's done in the past.
2.   Guessing based on why you would do it (your motives).
3.   Guessing based on certain beliefs about things and people.

Close Encounters with Beliefs

Some beliefs go beyond actual events in the child's life. To say Sam's playful noises really was his conspiring against mom and dad on ways to be bad that day, is way out in left field. These are called "irrational beliefs." Irrational beliefs come from unknown events. They construct an empire of assumptions about why events happen and how you should react toward them. In part irrational beliefs come from days of your own childhood, raised by parents who indoctrinated these very same beliefs into meal and prayer. Now, as an adult, certain irrational beliefs take control over your own behavior or become the eyes through which you judge other people's behavior.

Years ago researchers of irrational beliefs compiled 11 major beliefs and then added several more for a total list of the top 29 most common beliefs people have. Read these items below and respond "true" or "false" to each statement:

1.   An adult should be loved or approved by almost everyone for virtually everything he or she does.

2.   I should be thoroughly competent, adequate and achieving in all respects.

3.   Certain people are bad, wicked or villainous and should be severely blamed and punished for their sins.

4.   It is terrible, horrible, and a catastrophe when things are not going the way I would like them to go.

5.   Human unhappiness is caused by things beyond my control. I have no ability to control my sorrows or to rid myself of negative feelings.

6.   If something is bad or dangerous, I should be terribly occupied with and upset by it.

7.   It is easier to avoid facing many difficulties and responsibility than to be self–disciplined.

8.   The past is all important and that because something once strongly affected my life, it should always do so.

9.   People and things should be different from the way they are. Because of this, it is catastrophic if perfect solutions are not found for problems.

10.   Maximum human happiness can be achieved by doing nothing but waiting around.

11.   It is horrible if I make mistakes.

12.   It is in my best interest to try to be good at everything I do, or at least to pretend that I know everything.

13.   It pays off in the short and long run that the less I disclose about myself, the better off I will be.

14.   Let's face it, I am a victim of circumstances. My life is basically at the mercy of outside forces. As if somebody up there in the heavens threw a pair of die and said, "this is how so and so will live today!"

15.   The worse crime in the world is that everybody but me is always happy.

16.   One way of avoiding unpleasant situations is to keep my anger inside.

17. No matter what the outcome is, I should feel guilty if I do my own thing and others are upset by it.

18. Friendships are critical to my well–being. So, I should make sure that I please other people and that they like and approve of me.

19. Remember that my opinion should be definite. Be right, and show others that my opinion is better than their opinions.

20. If I want to be happy, I should work for my happiness.

21. It pays off for me to never take risks on anything.

22. I should always be independent and self–sufficient.

23. If I avoid problems and bad situations they will disappear in time.

24. I should always be perfect.

25.   Stereotypes tell me a lot about people. I can draw general conclusions about people from their statements and actions.

26.   Not all people come from the same backgrounds. So, it makes sense to think some people are better than other people.

27.   My behavior serves as tools for making an impression on people. I should be sure to perform well so others will like me.

28.   It make sense to believe most of what I hear.

29.   My own peculiar thoughts always are to be taken seriously.

How many statements did you rate as "true?" Many of these statements reflect your "beliefs." A belief, again, is something about what *should be* or *ought to be*. "Shoulds" and "oughts" enter your vocabulary to explain why children did things. "Musts" are another belief. "They *must* do this," or "he *must* wash the dishes tonight. Must–type statements read a lot into children's actions by presuming he knows to behave the way you want him to that he is totally aware of every expectation of him.

Consider statement #4 on the True/False test. "It is terrible, horrible, and a catastrophe when things are not going the way I would like them to go." To an extent this statement is about real problems in life that ruin personal expectations. Getting to work on time is ruined when your child eats slowly, spills milk on himself or has tantrums. It makes you angry, perhaps even causes arguments. All these reactions are common and make the situation unpleasant.

Whether this unpleasant situation really is catastrophic is another story. Why should it be a catastrophe? Catastrophes are earthquakes, hurricanes, tornadoes, deaths, accidents and emergencies involving natural disasters. Calling a disappointment or unwanted change in plans a "catastrophe" means the change causes a disaster. You can think it is a catastrophe, but it really isn't. There are few actual catastrophes in daily situations with children. Nothing is catastrophic about a disappointment or inconvenience in life unless you make it one. You may like a world free of disappointment and inconvenience, but it's rare. Your expectations describe how you would like the world to be, not how it *must be*.

Irrational beliefs drift off from real events and cause distortions the more serious you are about "musts," "shoulds" and "oughts." For this reason every answer on that true/false questionnaire was "false." All the statements are irrational beliefs. For example, take being independent (#22). Many people believe they must do everything themselves. That depending on other people is a sign of weakness. Of course, this belief is false because people are not skilled in every aspect of life and sooner or later need another person for something.

Perfection is another one (#24). We all would like to avoid mistakes. But they happen anyway. Striving for absolute perfection seems a hardy goal because it means hard–working, self–discipline. High achievers all agree that first in reaching your potential is minimizing your errors. So, doesn't perfection seems a realistic goal?

No. It doesn't. Real problems enter the scene with perfectionism. Let's take a moment or two to describe problems with this belief and how it terribly injures your parenting. Take, for instance, our friend Sally. Sally works at a bank and tries very diligently to leave the house in order every morning. Her two children are loud and messy and disrupt this plan of a clean house. Every morning, without fail, she follows the children around, picking up after them and overly correcting their mistakes. Sally says this correction keeps them tidy and makes them aware of her expectations. Is Sally right about this?

One way to figure it out is by asking, how is Sally perfectionistic? Sally persists with cleaning and over–cleaning primarily because of two reasons. First, is because she hates a messy house or is fearful of criticism by others who might see the messy house. Second, that she is so embarrassed, annoyed or angry about the mess that cleaning will instantly relieve her aggravation. In both cases Sally's effort can be explained as *avoidance or escape behavior*.

Avoidance is her being so afraid of rejection, disapproval, criticism or what may ensue in the event of a messy house, that she exerts labor to *prevent* even the slightest chance of it happening. Escape is her experiencing the humiliation around others and doing everything possible to *get out of the situation quickly*.

Anticipating the worst, Sally may be impatient if she cannot clean the house or discovers her children ruined her cleaning efforts. This is not because Sally takes pride in cleaning, in having a neat house or even because she likes to be efficient. Sally's driving urge to clean operates on intense *fear* that awful consequences will lead to impending doom if that house is a mess. And that's the way perfectionism always affects people. If you find yourself obsessive about cleaning, or doing things without any errors, almost to where a single error seems catastrophic, ask yourself, what you are afraid of? Are you afraid of:

1. Looking stupid?
2. Looking incompetent?
3. Hating yourself?
4. Losing friends?
5. Receiving criticism or punishment?
6. Feeling inadequate?
7. Feeling worthless?

Any of these reactions show that you are scared of how people may treat you in the event of mistakes. Do you notice, feeling this fear, that mistakes you cannot avoid are handled around people by doing one or more of the following?

1. You apologize and apologize for the mistake.
2. You feel compelled to do something for the person who caught your mistake.
3. You feel defensive and possibly argumentative.
4. You make excuses or feign sickness.
5. You insult yourself in front of the person.
6. Your words and actions make another per son feel superior to you.

Feeling devastated by mistakes scares people into a frenzy of searching for a local escape hatch rather than face the uncertain fate of confrontation. To confront, to deal directly with your errors, means directly acknowledging you cannot do everything right. You cannot cross every "T" and dot every "i." Nobody can. And raising children creates constant disruptions and roadblocks that make it nearly impossible to purify your error–free life. Sally's anger at her kids, in other words, was not because of what the kids did wrong, but what she did wrong. She pretended every morning, like every day, *should be, must be, and ought to be* started with a clean room, a clean house, and perfect order.

Sally forgot to realize that no matter how clean, how perfect the house looked, somebody inevitably will make comments anyway. Criticism could be about the kitchen, even if the kitchen looks immaculate. Criticism could be about the bedrooms, even if every bed is made, curtains washed, and floor vacuumed. It doesn't matter. Totally preventing criticism is impossible and hours upon hours that are spent anticipating criticism simply misses the main point. The point is that if Sally and others just dealt with people directly, by confronting them and accepted normal mistakes, needs for perfection would fade.

Parents trapped by their own insulated fears of mistakes are bound to make assumptions. The way out of this trap is a stiff upper lip and confidence that you can deal with natural events as they really are, not as you wish them to be.

Getting Rid of Assumptions

Saying farewell to assumptions sounds easier than it appears at first. Like any habits, assumptions from your early childhood glue onto your personality and it feels very strange to let them go. In fact, many parents describe the feeling of releasing assumptions as putting their thoughts up for adoption. Once gone, the new way of perceiving children feels even more strange. In fact, as you learn and practice different ways of looking at your children, expect the following personal reactions:

1. It will feel like the wrong thing to do.
2. It will feel forced or mechanical.
3. It will feel embarrassing.
4. It will feel like your children "know what you're doing."

Strange at first, changes you make to counter assumptions represent the healthiest improvement in your life. To begin, remember the 3 golden rules to assumption control, also known as IRS (not Internal Revenue Service). First is *isolate* the assumption. Second is *return* to natural events. Third is *select* how to react.

Isolate the Assumption

Moments after Jordan talks back to you, your face feels flushed, as burning resentment builds up inside of you. What should you do ? First, isolate the assumption. *What am I reading into this? What do I think is going on here?* The most obvious is that Jordan should not say that to me. His behavior is awful, horrible and must be punished. Yet the assumption goes beyond his actual behavior and so now ask yourself the following:

Why is my assumption wrong?

Why should I not take it personally?

Here is why your assumption is wrong. You do not know all the facts surrounding Jordan's remarks. Is he angry, upset, annoyed, deprived? Details regarding his behavior are unclear, lost or not obvious. Unless you have key facts about his behavior, dismiss the assumption because it lacks validity. Why he did what he did doesn't matter until you know the facts. Get the facts first.

By the same token, how do you know his behavior is your fault? Is it something you did wrong or does his behavior pertain to something else? Not taking it personally means that you put immediate distance between yourself and his events. Look at his behavior like a spectator sitting way above the playing field in the bleachers. There you can objectively turn away from it without feeling part of the action. Remove yourself as a player and become a bystander, hearing yourself say. . ."it's only events. His behavior is only events."

Return to Natural Events

Detachment is a process of turning off needless emotions while in the trenches. Now, look at the behavior as a geologist looks at rocks. She doesn't read between the lines and abstractly guess that the rock is small, old or light. She instead bases these comments on directly observing exact things about the rock—its color, shape, size, and so forth. The same applies for children. Look at concrete features about their behavior such as the following:

What things happened right before this bad behavior?

What things happened as he did the bad behavior?

Was the bad behavior verbal, physical or both?

What things happened right after this bad behavior?

What you're doing is sticking with the facts of behavior. Or beginning to search for facts instead of simply guessing what they are. Facts give shape and form on the parameters of behavior as well as keep you at an even keel. What if you discover Jordan's behavior was due to these reasons?

Right before his behavior: He broke his shoelace, and dropped his cookie.

As he did his behavior: He screamed, yelled and was attention–seeking.

Nature of behavior: He was mainly verbal.

Right after his behavior: You almost did, but at the last moment did not give him attention for the behavior.

Knowing these details gives you a special edge over his behavior and strengthens your self–control. You also realize his behavior actually had nothing to do with you, and that facts gained from watching him closely were different from your assumptions.

Select How to React

How should you react? Just because you wear objective glasses and can stop yourself from assumptions doesn't mean you also stop your emotions. Emotions heated by the generator of anger, contempt and feelings of parent exploitation can bust through the best intentions of mice and men.

Jordan might get your wrath and fury just out of your old habits. Even if you "now know better than to do that." One way to avoid this mistake is selecting a new way to react.

The best reaction is either "no reaction" or something really different: Try positively attending to your child. Chapters 4 and 5 further introduce guidelines along these lines. For now, then, set your limits on two types of parental coping strategies. First, detach yourself from the disruptive behavior either by leaving the room temporarily or focusing intensely on some activity such as watching television or being busy. Second, once the behavior settles down and initial bursts of emotion subside, walk up to your child and give him attention.

Again:

First, detach yourself by involvement in something else.

Second, give attention to calm, quiet and appropriate behavior.

The biggest mistake is thinking your child is wise to your new strategy and will out–smart your efforts by persisting or calling you on it. Even verbally articulate children who say "I see what you're doing...you're ignoring me...and it's not going to work..." are still victims of your method. They recognize differences in your behavior but are oblivious to why you have changed and what those changes will do to them.

Rest assured, then, your efforts remain largely a secret kept from your child's full awareness.

CHAPTER 4

4–Steps To Stop Tantrums

Many parents, like yourself, have come up with new and "hot ideas" on how to control kids' tantrums. But few ideas pass the test of lasting success. It's not because the ideas are wrong. But because steps are missing. Now, finally, you can rest easier knowing the inside secrets of tantrum control.

All you need to do is follow 4 simple steps. Just 4 simple steps decreases your son's or daughter's anger. Surest way to make all four work is to :

ALWAYS BE CONSISTENT

I am quite certain you are the consistent type. You want to do things the same way each time. But this is not always possible because of interruptions.

So, try your best. Don't be distracted by tantrums. Remember: You will now have skills other parents do not have!

Picture yourself a week from now. You've done it! Control over tantrums. You will feel great by following the four steps clearly given in this chapter. Ready? Here we go.

STEP 1: Never Take Tantrums Personally

Successful parents know something you are about to know, that mean and nasty tantrums are just outbursts. Nothing more. Outbursts gain your attention. Meaning, tantrums worsen the more you react or give attention to them.

Chapter 3 talked about this point in detail. Children of all ages who tantrum want something. They want your attention. Attention is a very common selfish need. All children have this need. But how your child shows it, by tantrums, is the wrong way. So, you will teach your child good way to get attention. This means:

DON'T:

1.   Read into or analyze tantrums. Just accept that they are for attention.

2.   Explain tantrums with adult reasons. Children think like children, not like adults. They aren't "testing you," "teasing you," or "pushing your buttons." None of these are true.

3.   Think tantrums are because of something "you did wrong." You are a fine parent and tantrums occur anyway.

Stick with the tantrum itself. Read nothing into it. It's only for attention and it feeds off of your attention. The angrier you get, the worse is the tantrum. It always is this way.

When tantrums start, your best offense is defense. Hold back from "reprimands" and from explaining why a tantrum is bad. Your reasons will only fuel a steady fire of tantrums. Here is what to do instead. Follow Step 2.

STEP 2: Ignore the Outburst

You're probably thinking, "Ignore it?" I've tried that before and it doesn't work at all. Doesn't that only make things worse?

Yes and no. There is a real good reason to ignore tantrums. Attention you give to tantrums increases tantrums. Removal of attention slows down the outbursts. That makes the outburst tolerable. In a second we'll show you what happens to tantrums when they are ignored. But first, here's the real way to ignore tantrums:

IGNORE MEANS:

1. No looking, pointing, glaring or talking.
2. No explaining, yelling, or satisfying what he or she wants.
3. No letting them lay or pull on you, on your clothing.
4. No warnings, threats, promises, or signs of affection (hugs, kisses, etc.)
5. No signs of anger, resentment, or physical punishment.

Ignoring begins and ends with patience. You'll know exactly how long to ignore tantrums. That's where Step 3 comes in.

STEP 3:   Look For the Burst

What burst? Until parents try ignoring, they won't believe it. But it's true. Kids work harder for attention. Kids get attention faster the more effort they put into tantrums.

Just because you ignore the tantrum, it doesn't mean your child knows what you are doing. He or she doesn't know. It's normal for children to think you'll give them attention, just as you used to do. But they are wrong. The longer you hold back, notice what happens:

"Behavior Always Gets Worse—Increases— Before it Gets Better."

You see, tantrums at first "burst" out in mild to severe form. Then the tantrum cools down as time passes. Not in 3–4 hours. But very soon, in a matter of minutes. How long you wait for tantrums determines how short they are in the future. Poor patience inspires worse tempers. Good patience guarantees tantrums will diminish. Just ignore the outburst for as long as it lasts.

But wait a minute, that temper is getting worse! And he's getting away with it!

Don't be fooled. Even escalating tempers happen for good reasons. Awful yelling, screaming, and stumping up and down takes a toll on your nerves. It does on everybody's nerves. Anger, snappy comments, and name–calling even looks like your child is getting away with murder. *How dare he say that to me? After everything I do for him..why that son of a* .... Hold up. Don't lose it yet. Remember how important it is not to take personally your child's behavior, however rotten and offensive it is. Tantrums whirl into outrageous forms as your child reaches the "peak" or highest point of the burst. During a peak be ready to see these things happen:

1.   Ranting and raving at a high pitch.
2.   Calling you foul names.

3.   Threatening to destroy or ruin household property.

4.   Actually destroying household property.

5.   Running outside or threatening to run outside.

6.   Holding his breath.

7.   Excessive crying and coughing.

8.   Hitting you, your spouse, a sibling, or another friend.

Foul words and threats of property destruction usually put you over the edge. *It's one thing to listen to nonsense, but God help them if they abuse me or ruin my house.* Wrong. You're reading too much into it again. Nasty profanity shouted in a tantrum must be ignored so that your child gets the hint that it will not draw attention. One dead–eye look back at your child can ruin ignoring and accidentally teach him to go through this whole tantrum again next time you ignore him. And you don't want that to happen.

What if he kicks the wall, or knocks down your antique vase? Ready to kill, are you? STOP! Abrupt anger is exactly the juice keeping this battery alive. The danger with anger or correction of property threats is this: You'll literally teach your child that this is what he must do to assure mom's and dad's attention. Instead of learning that hurting furniture is bad, your child learns another lesson. A more bizarre lesson. One that takes much longer to correct later. The lesson is that communication with mom and dad starts and ends with doing things that make them yell.

So What Do I Do?

Here is what to look for and how to handle common problems in a burst:

1.   Tantrum happens in same order.
      What to do: Ignore it.
2.   Tantrums turns to verbal abuse.
      What to do: Ignore it and leave the room.
3.   Tantrum turns to physical abuse.
      What to do: Ignore it, remove breakable items from the room.
4.   Tantrum destroys physical property.
      What to do: Remove property, remove potential hazards, and don't speak to your child during the burst.

5. Tantrum is harmful to other kids.
    What to do: Give sympathy to injured or hurt persons. Say nothing to tantruming child.

6. Tantrum attracts other children's attention.
    What to do: Distract other children away from tantrum child.

7. Tantrum causes self–injury.
    What to do: Treat the injury but say nothing to your child.

8. Tantrum lasts longer than 30 minutes.
    What to do: Figure out who gave attention to tantrums. Stop the leak before it ruins your efforts.

9. Tantrum gets kids or siblings to laugh at your child.
    What to do: Promise the other kids a treat or reward for ignoring the tantrum and doing something else.

10. Tantrum is so bad you call it quits.
    What to do: Hold on there! That's a deadly no, no! Never give in. Even if you think you've taken all you can. Here's why you can't give in:

Tantrums you work so hard to ignore might get twice as bad just by giving in to them.

If you've waited this long, wait longer. You can out–wait your child. Believe me, there's a nasty price for giving in. All the tantrums up to when you give in—verbal and physical abuse—everything will repeat itself next time you try to ignore the outburst. So, take my word, count sheep or leave the room but hold out until the behavior fades. You'll be glad you waited and it will make Step 4 easier to do.

STEP 4: When Tantrum Fades

This is the fun part. Tantrums do slow down. And when they do we can't hold a grudge against the child. Here's what to do when your son or daughter calms down after an outburst:

After the Outburst:

1.   Don't talk about the tantrum episode.

2.   Ask your child to do a very simple task like touch his nose or name an object or bring something to you. Let them know a hug, kiss

or some affection or kind words will follow for being good.

3.   If your child refuses, just let it pass. It's no big deal.

4.   If he or she repeats the tantrum, *return to Step 1.*

5.   If he or she comes over but is huffy, just let it pass.

6.   If your child does the simple task, then starts the tantrum, again, *return to Step 1.*

Easy steps happen when you make them happen. Follow Steps 1 through 4 next time tantrums begin and see the difference your efforts have upon your child.

Yes, yes. That's all fine and good. But what if tantrums keep on going?

Good question. Glad you asked. Tantrums run a regular course of highs and lows usually ending up on a low note. But kids ages 3 to 10 and even into adolescence may have tantrums so loud and so frequent, and for so many years that ignoring is not enough. Temper bursts go through the roof with ear–shattering octaves of shouts, wall–bangings, hyperactivity, and heavy property destruction. Behaviors this severe didn't start yesterday and happen everywhere and anywhere. At home, at school, at church, synagogue, and always–*the grocery store*. Will this 4–step method do the trick?

No, not exactly. Tantrums put under control by the 4–step approach are persistent verbal attacks plus some physical action. Loudness is also not a problem. That's because verbal behavior is always easier for change than is other action behavior. And when action is brutal, injurious, or dangerous to others in ways causing serious household damage, steps must be followed beyond the 4–step approach. That's when it's time to ask, *hmm, do I or my child need therapy?* Chapter 9 answers that question for you.

Final Action To Take

The opera never finishes until the fat lady sings. With tantrum control, a days' job is never over until the final step is in place. That step deals with applying this 4–step approach in many different situations. It's all part of *transferring what your child learns at home to other people and places.* Silly as this may sound, no more tantrums in the house does not guarantee tantrums disappear everywhere else your child goes. Especially if tantrums did take place in other places or around certain people.

Tactics to take to assure your hard work pays off are simple. Make a point of having your child in the following situations where tantrums might pop up, and you can be there armed with the 4–step approach:

1.   Around peers.
2.   Around stores.
3.   Around restaurants.
4.   Around relatives
5.   Around grandma and grandpa.
6.   Around new babysitters.
7.   Around your friends and families.
8.   Around church or synagogue.

And let new people take care of your children now that their tantrums are under control. Stop protecting them from people, or protecting people from your children. It's time to test out your skills on caring friends, family, and babysitters who can watch the children while you, alone, or with your spouse take a night out.

Okay, so how do I know this works?

You'll know. Signs of success spring forth in living color from all directions and make you feel the happiest parent alive. Look for signs of excellent progress if the following occur:

1.   Number of daily tantrums decreases to 1 or 2 times.
2.   Length of burst for each tantrum is shorter, around 1–5 minutes.
3.   Severity of burst for each tantrum is less, no more than some yelling, maybe angry words, and minor feet stomping.

4.   Your child stops his tantrums, then is quiet for a second. Then asks you for a kiss or something to do as if repeating step 4.

5.   Bursts at other high–risk places are fewer, hardly at all.

6.   You're own yelling and anger happens fewer times.

7.   You realize how much fun your child is to be with.

8.   You hear wonderful compliments from others on how well behaved he is. This is especially meaningful from people who knew your child in his temper tantrum days.

These bright signs of progress are great feedback on your work. But there is an ugly truth behind all the glitter. Tantrums are like "trash." You can remove every morsel of trash from the house and still have just as much, if not more the next week. It all depends on how much garbage you go through. It's like giving attention to tantrums. That's a garbage reaction.

Reacting the wrong way after years of a habit is difficult to change. Mistakes and old habits occasionally slip out no matter how masterful you become at the 4–step approach. It's not a crisis. And you're not expected to be perfect the first time, second time, or even the third time around. Just do the best you can. That's all that counts.

CHAPTER 5

What To Do When Your Child Says "NO!"

Bobby doesn't clean his room.

Sally never sets the table.

Mary leaves her wet clothes out.

Harold doesn't brush his teeth.

"Darn kids, they just don't follow instructions." Parents say this when their children do not comply. Compliance means your child does something you want done. More and more parents believe compliance is part of maturity. That kids automatically do things for you at a certain age. If they don't comply, that stage will pass and a new, more compliant stage begins. Of course, this idea is a myth.

This chapter is on simple methods to teach your child how to follow instructions. That is, what to do when your child says **N O !** Minding, or "following instructions," is at the heart of good parent–child relations. An important part of compliance is understanding what exactly goes on during compliance. Let's first consider what compliance really is, and then learn the steps for putting it in action.

Really, What is Compliance?

Bruce left his bicycle outside in the rain. His mother told him to put it away, but he didn't do it. Bruce is definitely noncompliant. He should know better, shouldn't he?

Yes and no. We must be careful not to blame kids for what they *should* or what they *shouldn't* know to do. They're not adults and do not think like adults. Adults have more experiences, better memory, and know how to follow instructions. Children lack this background.

"Children are not adults and do not think like adults."

Following instructions, then, involves two parts. First is (a) *what* a parent says. Second is (b) what the child has the *ability* to do. Usually parts (a) and (b) fit together so that what you ask for connects with what your child does. But never assume this is true. Many things go on in between your instruction and when your child responds. Consider these factors, for instance:

1. What is the parent doing at the time?
2. What is the child doing at the time?
3. Where are parent and child located at the time?

What is the parent doing at the time? This refers to what you and your child are doing before or during an instruction. Kids busy with some toy or activity have "competing activities." Parents busy with work or a task are under an urge to keep doing that task. Interruption of that urge gets you very angry, impatient, and you might yell. Asking for things when you are under an urge makes you less tolerant to mistakes. It also makes you in a hurry to demand compliance.

Wonder what it takes to be under an urge? It takes being under a time limit to do something, not knowing how to do it, or discovering obstacles in the way. All three things are there. (More on this later in Chapter 6.)

Where are parent and child located? It matters where you and your child are when giving instructions. A parent in one room cannot expect a playing child in another room to hear you. Make sure your child is nearby or in listening range.

Now that you have this background, you're ready for the best part. That of following two easy steps for children to mind you better.

STEP 1: If ——> Then

Let's begin at the beginning. Giving instructions is a two–step process. First you ask your child to do something. That's the easy part. When asking the favor, promise him a reward in return. Parts of this instruction are real specific and most of you already use many of these parts. Follow these parts in the order they appear:

Step 1. Tell your child:

1.   *What* you want him to do.
"Burt, I want you to pick up the dirt."

2.   *When* you want him to do it.
"Burt, pick up the dirt right now."

3.   *How* you want him to do it.
"Burt, pick up the dirt in this way."

4.   *Where* you want him to do it.
"Burt, pick up the dirt over here."

5.   *What he can get* for doing it.
"If you. . . .Then I will. . . ."

Let's say a word or two about the last part or #5, about "if. . . .then... " Simple rewards are things immediately around you and easy to give your child. How about hugs, kisses, funny smiles or faces or tickles, or even horsey–back rides? Figure out ahead of time what your child really enjoys that is fast and lots of fun.

There are easy ways to find rewards for kids. Consider these guidelines for starters:

1. **Promise your child a few minutes to do things he enjoys himself.**
2. **Promise your child a few minutes alone with you or your spouse.**
3. **Promise your child a few minutes describing some activity he enjoys.**
4. **Promise your child some object, event he can play with right after compliance.**

Rewards fall into basically four categories. These include *material things, privileges and activities, social events,* and *tokens.* Material things include food and other desirable objects. Privileges and activities cover trips, games and so on. Social events overlap a bit with privileges but deal with more intimate or personal activities. Tokens are forms of money or gifts that are exchangeable for other rewards.

Now make up your own list of possible rewards for each child in your family. Place the reward under headings like we did in Table 5.1

Table 1
Menu of Reinforcers for Infants and Children

- -

Material Things	*Privileges & Activities*
toys	finger paint
snacks	smelling flowers
dessert	trip to zoo
shiny objects	ride in stroller
ice cream	trip to park
soft, fuzzy toys	play with friends
humming	play on swingset
singing	family night
candy	night at grandparents
soft drinks	ricking horse
	video games
	eating out
	play with clay
	play in sandbox
	play with magnets

Social Events	*Tokens*
cooing	money
hugs/kisses	stars
verbal praise	allowance
winks	food
eye contact	points
boasting about him	stickers
playing hand games	
pictures	
handshake	scratch/sniff
ask their opinions	
wrestling	
bouncing on knee	
tickling	

Once you get started on Step 1 you may discover something. Your child doesn't just do as you say. In fact he does one of the following. He or she:

Says "No!"
Remains Silent
Gets Angry
Runs Away

Yells a lot
Starts Debating

When these things happen the best approach is to ignore them. Just let them happen and apply your strategy discussed in Chapter 4 on tantrums. Now begins Step 2.

STEP 2: Look for Delay and Competing Behaviors

Look for things your child is doing that distract him from the instruction. You'll find them. They're around. It can be anything from watching television to a toy to just sitting in front of the fan. But it's there and keeping your child from doing what you want him or her to do. Here's what to do now:

Steps on eliminating competing behaviors.

1. **Find and remove the competing thing and then repeat the instruction from Step 1. OR**

2. Find and remove the competing thing and then promise to return it after your child complies.

The other thing to watch out for is "delay" behavior. This is your child's arguing or negotiating or just sitting there doing nothing. Delay means he will postpone doing the task you asked him to do. You can overcome this trap by following the same steps you used for the competing things.

But Oh, no! You wake up the next morning after laboring through these strategies and discover an awful thing:

It Still Doesn't Work!!!

Why, oh, why is this happening? Frustration mounts when you try both steps and still feel it isn't working. But relax. Sit down. Don't worry. There really are good reasons why Steps 1 and 2 might fail. A careful memory of them will keep you ahead of the game. Here are seven reasons why things may go sour:

1. Your child does not understand

the instructions.

2. Your child doesn't know how to do the task you're asking of him.
3. Your child lacks an important part of the instruction (words).
4. Your child cannot physically do the task.
5. Your child is afraid to ask for help and simply doesn't do it.
6. Your child is afraid that bad things will follow for doing what you want.
7. Your child does not find your rewards very rewarding.

It's wrong to get mad at your child without considering these possibilities. Remember that it is easier for you to follow instructions than it is for your child to follow instructions. They lack all the adult wisdom and experience you have and only know limited information. Assuming they think and act like you do, and should follow instructions like you do, will only get you mad. And it isn't worth getting mad about.

Be honest with yourself on why your child doesn't mind you. If every day is the same thing

"He doesn't listen to a single word I say!" Then here are the things to troubleshoot before jumping to Steps 1 and 2.

Be a troubleshooter not a troublemaker. Ask yourself:

1. Am I giving attention to "delay" behavior?
2. Am I asking him to do too much? Should my requests be for small amounts instead of large amounts?
3. Am I arguing too much?
4. Have I been too inconsistent?

The real test is consistently and patiently using these steps even when you think they fail. Remember that compliance is like an onion. At the core is obedience. But getting to the core involves peeling off layer after layer of delay and competing behaviors. You can do it. Believe me, you can. Plenty of parents achieve this goal all the time. And even when all else fails, there's still more hope ahead.

More Troubleshooting

Following instructions is something you teach your children to do. Not something the kids instantly pick up as a part of being a child. It doesn't come with the package. They have to learn it—step by step. When your kids still do not mind you, after following the steps above, there are other reasons to consider. Some of these reasons parents can work through pretty easily. Other reasons are stickier and take more time and effort.

When These Steps Are Not Working

Stubbornly refusing to do what you ask is part of the learning process. Anger, resentment, and even name–calling put you into shock but are minor compared to some problems that crop up without parents realizing it. Here are some common problems that interfere with and ultimately sabotage following instructions. Solutions to them are also provided.

"My Child Still Doesn't Care About My Feelings!" (The Insensitive Child)

Not only does he lack feeling for your needs, but feelings are absent for everybody's needs. Your son or daughter is without an emotional bone in their body—never thinks about how people feel, or if their actions might upset somebody. Brad, for example, jumps in front of the television set when the whole family is watching it. Even if "we all ignore him, and his burst is over, he still rudely interrupts as if we were not even there."

Why does Brad do this? Is he really a conniving manipulator filled with ruthless instincts? No, not exactly. Brad is a boy who after years of attention–seeking actions and getting away with it, has lost a special reaction called "shame." He has no guilty conscience. He feels no remorse. Actions impulsively occur one right after the other without any sensitivity to who is inconvenienced by the actions. Loss of guilt means he developed a sense of "I can do anything" from all the people who gave into his wishes and needs when he acted out. Now "I can do anything" takes on larger proportions. No more small time robberies. No more stealing one cookie from the cookie jar. Now it's 5 cookies, everyday, even after he promises and promises not to take it. Promises mean nothing. He doesn't care who he hurts. They are not important.

Letting this disrespect toward people continue has grave consequences. These can be the makings of a Jim Jones or Charles Manson—but not for many years. On the immediate front is your child taking risks that are excessive for his age. Consider a four year old boy talking about sex to a four year old girl. Or, a seven year old girl saying she can do anything she wants in her house when the babysitter is there, including drink from the liquor cabinet. Extreme cases? Not all the time. It depends on how successful kids have been in their risks. Risks also take on a selfish attitude. The only one who benefits is the risk–taking child.

One way around this problem is *making your child sensitive to what people feel or think*. This seems contradictory. So much of this book repeats the message for parents to ignore what other adults think of you and do the right thing. So, why should children pay attention to feelings? Here's the answer: Because they don't know how to. Oversensitive adults pay attention to people's feelings too much. They need to cut back on their fears. But insensitive or grossly disrespectful children literally do not have this skill in their day to day habits. It's not a matter of too little or too much. It simply doesn't exist.

So, teaching sensitivity is the solution. You can accomplish this goal by doing the following steps. When your child physically or verbally does something that is excessive or is mean to another child (except during a "burst"),

1.   Tell your child to apologize to the person. Then have your child say complimentary or nice things about the person.

2.   Spoon–feed the exact words on what your child should say. For example, "Now, Bruce, tell Susan you are sorry for what you said. (Bruce mumbles "sorry"). Good. Now, tell her you think she is pretty and you like her dress." Have your child repeat your words exactly or as close as possible.

3.   Tell your child to do something––even minor––for that person.Things your child can do vary from helping the person with a chore to creating new efforts that take the apology above and beyond the call of duty. Let your child write her a 3–line letter or say into the tape–recorder that he is sorry or why she is pretty. If the victim is a sibling,

let your child clean that sibling's room or do one of the chores the sibling usually does.

4.   Resistance to saying "I'm sorry" or "do the corrective task" is just left alone like ignoring a tantrum. Never force this behavior or you will have more trouble on your hands. However, while you ignore your child's stubbornness, the victim (sibling or friend) gets to benefit from it. Ask that sibling or friend to do an easy chore or task lasting only seconds or a few minutes.

Once done, reward the sibling or friend, with big thank you's for respecting adults and being cooperative. Your stubborn child will watch rewards received for a different type of behavior. He may want to apologize or do the task after watching that sibling or friend get the reward. That's okay. Let it happen, and then give the same reward to your child.

WARNING, WARNING

Always remember not to give any type of attention to your child while your child is yelling, screaming or tantruming. That will spoil your earlier efforts to let this behavior fade away.

"My Child is Lying to Me!" (*Lying*)

The "I don't care" attitude or actions connect with some other behavior, when your child lies to you. This hurts deep inside your gut. After all, children are supposed to love and respect their parents, right? After all that time, effort and patience parenting this child, lying feels like a serious betrayal. A let down beyond belief. "How could my child do that to me?" What did I do to deserve this?" *Nothing. Lying occurs because your child is afraid to tell you the truth. It's too scary. You may get angry or punish your child, and in his youthful perception, that would be catastrophic!* Children who are insensitive to parents readily skirt the truth and avoid punishment. This amounts to lying. And it happens for the same reason every time. The parent–child cycle is the same.

Did you ever do this to your child? Something rotten happens. So, you insist he tell you what happened. He tells you. But you become outraged. You raise your voice in anger, astounded he really did such a thing. You think your anger *proves* how bad this action was and that it should never happen again. Your anger is meant to pierce through his thick skin into his heart, so it stays with him the rest of his life.

And it does, but in the wrong way. Your attempt to make him understand the gravity of this bad thing he did backfired. Instead of realizing how bad the bad action was, your child received the wrong message from the airwaves. It came across like this, "Warning, Warning, never tell your mom and dad what really happened because they'll get angry." All your child learned is that disclosing the truth got him in trouble. Nothing connected about the immorality or badness of the action. On future occasions your child is wiser, more cautious and edits what you hear, or delays the facts long enough so that anger is delayed as well.

Yelling and screaming at the bad things your child told you instantly punishes his telling it to you. The verbal skill of sharing truth evaporates. So, when you ask her, "did you finish your chores today?" "Did you finish your homework?" "Did you take out the garbage?" All the replies of "of course I did, Dad" may be lies if your child is afraid to come straight with you.

Lying interferes with following instructions because it sends false messages to parents. And no matter how hard you use and re–use the steps shown earlier in the chapter, following instructions will not occur. Not until you work on the important problem first. Lying must be confronted. Here's how to do it.

Steps to Correct Lying Behavior

The main solution for lying is *not to make your child understand why lying is wrong. It is to re–teach him to tell you events that are true. Events parallel to real things. So, have your child describe the following details in this sequential order:*

1. **Neutral Descriptions About Things or Others.** Spend time with your child. Be sure you and your child share certain experiences that both of you saw, heard, felt, smelled or were part of. Fifteen minutes to one half hour after both of you had some experience, ask your child what he saw. You're asking about *neutral or very general things.* Nothing bad or particularly good. You were there with your child, so you can confirm the answers as true or false. For example, while riding in the car perhaps you both see a farm with cows and chickens. Ask, "Jenny, did that farm have cows and chickens?"

a.   A reply of "yes" should be followed with asking for more details. "What did the cows look like?" "Were there many of them?" After that, thank your child for answering you, and drop the discussion.

b.   A reply of "I don't know" should be followed with rephrasing the question. "Not sure, huh? Was there at least one cows there?" *Do not assume your child is lying just because she says "I don't know."*

c.   A reply of "no" or even more blatantly, "no, there were no cows and chickens," should be followed by rephrasing the questions like in #b. *Again, resist thinking your child is pulling a fast one over you. Just follow the steps.*

d.   A reply of "maybe, but I'm not sure" should be followed by rephrasing the question like in #b. If your child persists at not knowing the answer, let it go after a few tries.

e.   A reply of "yes, and there were foxes and lions there, too" should be handled a different way. Here your child inflates the story with details you know were absent. Say to your child, "I'm not sure the foxes and lions were there, but you're right about the chicken and cows." In other words, focus only on the accurate items your child remembered.

f.   A reply of "c'mon mom (dad), you know the answer" should be followed by "No, really, I forgot. And I know you have a good memory." Make sure your child replies at least a little bit to your questions. Full–length discussions about what both of you saw are not necessary.

g.   Repeat this first step of neutral descriptions several times a day until your child readily answers your questions without delay or changing the story. Let your child reply correctly up to three days in a row. Then go on to Step 2.

2.   *Positive Descriptions About Things or Others.* Now ask your child questions about positive things happening to other people or things he experienced. Experiences asked about are still things you also directly saw, heard, or were a part of. "Did you think your sister liked her birthday present this morning?" Both of you saw his sister excited about the gift, saying "Wow, great, Barbie's playhouse."

Now you want your child to says his sister was happy or liked her birthday present. Follow steps #a to f above on handling wrong answers. Repeat this second step of positive descriptions several times a day until your child readily answers your questions without delay or changing the story. Let your child reply correctly up to three days in a row. Then go on to Step 3.

3. *Negative Descriptions About Things or Others.* Now ask your child questions about negative things happening to other people. Accuracy here is very critical because it is the first time your child is telling you *bad things about something with some fear of what you might say in reply.* Again, things you ask about are what you experienced yourself first hand. Ask your child, for example, "what was your cousin doing to his mommy today that made his mommy upset?" Follow steps #a to f above on handling wrong answers. Repeat this third step of negative descriptions several times a day until your child readily answers your questions without delay or changing the story. Let your child reply correctly up to three days in a row. Then go on to Step 4.

4. *Neutral Descriptions About Himself* This is the first big step of truth–telling. When details return to your child's life. Ask your child questions about neutral things happening to her that you also directly experienced. Such questions as, "Charmane, did that pair of pants fit you that we tried on earlier today?" Of course, you already know the answer. Follow steps #a to f above on handling wrong answers. Repeat this fourth step of neutral descriptions several times a day until your child readily answers your questions without delay or changing the story. Let your child reply correctly up to three days in a row. Then go on to Step 5.

5. *Positive Descriptions About Himself* Now, ask your child questions about positive things happening to himself that you also directly experienced. "Well, was that fun seeing *Home Alone* at the movie theater today?" Follow steps #a to f above on handling wrong answers. Repeat this fifth step of positive descriptions several times a day until your child readily answers your questions without delay or changing the story. Let your child reply correctly up to three days in a row. Then go on to Step 6.

6. *Negative Descriptions About Himself* Now, ask your child questions about negative things happening to himself that you also directly experienced. This can be tricky, though. Be extra careful to speak softly, not angry or sound accusatory. Ask questions using the same friendly tone of voice you used in previous steps. Ask, for example, "did you use the last strip of toilet paper and forget to put a new one in?" Follow steps #a to f above on handling wrong answers. However, you must be aware of *the trap*. Do not fall into the trap of correcting your children for what they describe they did wrong. Just let it go and say "thank you."

Remember, correcting the bad things they admitted to you is how this problem of lying started in the first place. Please don't repeat it all over again. Repeat this sixth step of negative descriptions several times a day until your child readily answers your questions without delay or changing the story. Let your child reply correctly up to three days in a row. Then go on to Step 7.

7. *Neutral, Positive & Negative Descriptions About Himself Without You Being There.* We've finally made it. This is the last step. By this step your child's truth–telling is back into shape and

very little is left to do. It's a matter of fine tuning the engine now. Ask your child questions about neutral, positive, or negative things happening to himself that *you did not experience yourself.* You were not in the situation that you are asking about. Facts are entirely left up to your child. You have no way of verifying details as true or false. But based on how easily your child can now talk to you and share things you also experience, *there is a high probability that details told you are accurate.* Ask questions such as, "did you have a bad day at school?" Or, "your teacher called and told me you were sad, what was that all about?"

Follow steps #a to f above on handling wrong answers. Your questions can *sound like you know the truth, even though you really don't.* Repeat this last step several times a day until your child readily answers your questions without delay or changing the story. Let your child reply correctly up to three days in a row. Then periodically follow this step, but you can relax the number of questions each day. Let natural events in your life guide you on what you ask.

Any time your child does really great on one, two or three steps in a row but goofs up the fourth step, all is not lost. Just return to the last step he really did great on. Give it another 3 consecutive days of practice. Then move on to the next step. Never feel your child is a compulsive liar even when you *really think he is.* Lying is a behavior, like any other behavior, and can be changed with your help.

"My Child is Stealing from Me!" *(Stealing)*

Certain cardinal rules are not meant to be broken. This is one of them. Stealing. It's not okay. Stealing starts off with innocent borrowing, maybe your daughter forgot to get permission to take something. Maybe she didn't. Forgetting turns rapidly to *not caring what adults think when your child has an impulse to satisfy a need.* So, stealing from other people or from your own house still involves the same "I don't care" attitude and also is an advanced stage of lying. The two combined create a more vicious beast that is a little different to handle. Stealing takes three different forms:

1.   Stealing from parents and siblings
2.   Stealing from friends and relatives

3. Stealing from stores, school, or other places in community

Stealing from Parents and Siblings

"Give that back, that's mine!" Shouts of an angry sibling who discovered her CD was stolen from her room and is now in her brother's room. Why did he take it? Was it really something special? Something he needed more than anything else in the world? Probably not. In fact, temptation for stealing starts for simple reasons. Your child took the CD even if your child doesn't know what a CD is or how to use it. *But it was somebody else's property and looked interesting.* That is, your child observes somebody else, in this case, his sister, thoroughly enjoying her music while doing her homework. It looks stimulating, rewarding and enviable. Observed fun creates an urge to have that same fun. So, when she is not around and there is easy access to her room, he trespasses to her CDs and picks up one thinking he will instantly feel the fun his sister had.

But it doesn't really work that way. The CD doesn't generate fun for him and so your child looks for something else that *will be rewarding.* Since taking things is no longer foreign, risks are easier and he becomes more daring. Your child steals property guaranteed to give himself pleasure: *candy, money,* and *toys.* All three represent high excitement interests for small time house–theft.

And the worst part is exposing the thief. Parents quickly resort to all sorts of negative discipline on thievery because it feels right that your child should never, never do this again. But the following acts of punishment are worthless:

DON'T:

1. Just ground your child.
2. Send your children to their room without a meal.
3. Spank or yell at your child.
4. Leave your child out of family activities.
5. Tell friends and family how awful this behavior is in ear distance to your child.
6. Take money away from your child (adolescents).
7. Call the police or some authority to see how severe consequences of stealing really are.

INSTEAD, FOLLOW THESE STEPS IN THIS OR A SIMILAR ORDER:

1.   Have your child return the stolen property to yourself or sibling.

2.   Have your child apologize verbally and say "stealing is bad."

3.   After the property is returned, spent (money), consumed (food) or just gone, remove a desired or rewarding property from your child's room. Give that special property to the sibling your child stole from; or you keep the special property. Retain that special property for one to two days, then return it to your child.

4.   After removing the special property, have your child do something for the person he stole it from. If it was a sibling, have your child do a chore the sibling usually does, or run an errand. For yourself, the sky is the limit. As long as what your child does is something that is *easy, done immediately, not pleasant at all, and will not result in punishment.*

5.   Follow these steps the first time. The second time your child steals, make the labor more difficult. Third time, increase labor and

unpleasantness of task. Escalating effort and hatred of a task will more effectively discourage stealing than will any number of analytical talks with your child about why stealing is bad.

Stealing from Friends and Relatives

It's bad enough stealing from family, but when this habit goes outside the safe family unit, terror is felt. "He did what? When? My son did that? You must be kidding?" No, afraid not. It really happened. Then you feel angry. And anger burns inside like a raging fire until you lose your composure and take it out on your *bad child*. The hurt comes from being embarrassed that other people perceive your child as bad, untrustworthy or even banish her from their homes. Rejection of yourself is one thing; rejection of your child stings even worse. It's like being exiled from planet Earth. You feel devastated, humiliated, and want to hide your head in the sand. Well, don't be like an Ostrich yet. There's work to be done first.

Realize your child may not feel the same way. He moves to more daring thievery after successfully stealing at home. Especially if all your child received at home for stealing was harsh *punishment. Punishment only taught him to be more careful on when to steal or what to steal. Simple avoidance steps. Whereas putting him through effort and apologies forces your child to make up for the bad behavior (restitution).*

The second bad part of hearing what your child did is that it always is long after the fact—she stole 2 days ago, a week ago, or we just noticed the items missing when summer was over. Timing, in other words, is lousy and gives your child plenty of time feeling it was okay to take the property. But, of course, that's not the case. Here's what to do when you learn your child stole from a relative, your friend, or his friend.

DO THE FOLLOWING IN THIS OR A SIMILAR ORDER:

1.   Have your child return the property to the person's home along with one of his or her special properties sacrificed. It may be a Ninja Turtle, Barbie, GI Joe, Ghostbuster or any toy special to your child. It's gone. Now it's the property of the person your child stole from.

2.   Have your child apologize to the child he or she stole from, and that child's parents. If your

child can write, have your child also write an apology letter to that child and parents.

3.   Limit the time spent at that child's home. *Do not make the mistake of prohibiting that child to play there, unless the victim's parents prohibit it.* The reason is this: your child must face the same situation doing the correct behavior. If told never to play at that child's house again, your child never can practice his or her new (nonstealing) behavior in the situation. Learning not to steal requires your child to "return to the scene of the crime" but with appropriate behavior displayed. However, this doesn't mean your child is 100% trustworthy either. After he visits that child, ask your child exactly what they did, who they did it with, and what games they played with. If feeling any doubt, immediately call the parent of his or friend (relative) to verify the story.

Stealing from Stores , School ,and Other Places in the Community

There is nothing so vile than receiving a call from a local merchant who says your child just stole something. It feels like all your parenting lessons were for nothing. Deep betrayal of parental trust. That your child now has joined the ranks of *America's Most Wanted*. You imagine your child serving a life sentence in prison. Your imagination really takes off. Now you picture your child's offspring stealing, living like scum, inmates for life, or being put to death in the gas chamber. "Oh, God, have mercy on my misguided child!"

Well, the good news is that your six, seven or even twelve year old has a long ways before earning a free ride to State prison. It's a long, long, long ways away and probably never will happen. So, put your feet back on the ground and realize that petty theft from stores, schools and other places in the community is very common. Your child is not a kleptomaniac (compulsive stealer) just because she takes things. Observe instead *what they took, why they took it, whether the thing taken was needed, and whether there were any other ways of obtaining that item without stealing it.* Let's consider these questions closer:

1. *What they took.* Look very carefully at the object or property. Is it valuable? Easy to take? Breakable? How did they take it?

2.   *Why they took it.* Did they take it out of a dare, or was there a reason. Was it taken on impulse? Thought about it (premeditated)? Or did anybody coerce your child to take it?

3.   *Whether the thing taken was needed.* Does your child play or use these things? Are these items part of her life? What was the special attraction about this item in particular? What put your child under the urge to take this property at that moment?

4.   *Whether there were any other ways of obtaining that item without stealing it.* Was it an item you refused to buy? An item that is too expensive or inaccessible for some reason? Did your child know any other route of getting this property besides stealing it? Meaning, has he ever taken or tried another route but failed at it?

Figuring out what is going on is half the battle. You should also meet with the merchants or principals (of schools) to get the facts. Never just rely on one person's report or an incident file. So, presuming you now have all the facts, what do you do? Absolutely forbid your child to return to that place again? Hardly. Because if it is a school, your child must continue to go there. And if it is a store, one store is like any other store. Plus, you'll remember that returning to the scene of the crime and not stealing is the best way to improve behavior. So, there must be a better solution. How about these steps instead.

1.   Identify the stolen property.

2.   Have your child return that property with a letter of apology or saying "I'm sorry" to the property owner.

3.   If property owner agrees, have your child do some voluntary community service for them, lasting 1 to 2 hours depending on your child's age. Let the task be grossly unpleasant and physically tiresome. For example, in stores, have your child move or empty boxes (depending on child's age), sweep floors, or shovel snow along the sidewalk. In schools, have your child wash desks, wash chalk boards, do more assignments in the class he stole from, or some other dirty, smelly task.

(**WARNING:** It is worth repeating that removal of privileges, class or school suspension, in–school suspension or after school detention all fail miserably to correct stealing behavior. Children removed from class or school who do not learn to keep their hands off property *in the very same situation that motivated stealing,* will never change their behaviors.)

4.   If property owner disagrees with your plan or banishes your child from the store, assign unpleasant tasks for your child to do at home. But be clear that these gross tasks are the penalty for stealing. Hard, time–consuming and filthy tasks rapidly discourage subsequent interests in stealing.

Methods of *restitution* or "making up for the crime committed" are valid as long as you keep an eye on potential hazards. Hazards like your child getting the toy she wanted anyway, with or without stealing it, or her getting somebody else to do her filthy task. These interferences contaminate restitution. So, be prepared. Here is a list of possible problems that might creep up:

1.   Your child steals more property while doing the restitution. (If so, extend the restitution including worse tasks and more tasks around the house.)

2.   Your child does fine with restitution in one place, but in the meantime steals the same property from another owner. (If so, intensify the unpleasant tasks assigned, in each place he or she steals from.)

3.   Your child gets as a gift the same property she stole. (If so, return the gift.)

4.   Your child destroys the property stolen before you see it or have a chance to return it to its owner. (If so, forfeit one of your child's prized possessions to the owner or his family.)

5.   Your child stays "clean." But he gets another child or sibling to do the stealing for him or her. (If so, both must follow your strategy as if they committed the crime together.)

There is a point at which stealing can get out of control. Nobody likes to believe it, and saying, "okay, now that's a classic kleptomaniac" is risky.

It's a risk for the accuser, and a risk for you, the parents. You risk defending your child at the expense of overlooking what may be a very serious habit. So bad, in fact, that these initial methods of behavior control only touch the surface. Experienced child thieves may develop so many complex skills associated with stealing you may need a child specialist or therapist to dismantle the corrupt repertoire. But never fear, help is near. All you have to do is be willing to admit there is a problem when your efforts fail.

"My Child is a Perfectionist!" *(Perfectionism)*

There is another reason kids do not follow instructions. They may be so afraid of making mistakes if they do what you ask them to do, that kids just don't do it at all. Bruce was like that. He never did what his mother asked him to do. She said it politely—and he ignored her. She screamed––and he ignored her. She bribed him with goodies––and again he ignored her. Nothing worked. So, she concluded Bruce was too stubborn and had a mental illness.

Good news was that it was not a mental illness at all. Just fear. Bruce was afraid of his mother's reaction to mistakes when he did the things she requested. Take, for example, setting the table for dinner. Forks on the left side of the plate, knives on the right side, napkins underneath the fork, spoons adjacent to the knives, tea cups to the right of plate, salad plate on top of large plate, and napkin rings centered on plate. Got it? No, Bruce didn't get it. And every time he goofed up the order or re-arranged plates and forks it was wrong. Dead wrong. At least that's how his mother made him feel for this mistake.

Bruce felt a toxic shame for setting the table wrong. Next time he set the table he moved slower, almost rigidly, trying to get all silverware and dishes in the exact place. But time and time again errors showed up that infuriated his mother and scared Bruce into thinking that he just could not get the hang of this task. So, he stopped doing it altogether. When *he does do it, or is forced to do it, he is very attentive to details and must get things in precise order or else it seems horrible, catastrophic and deadly.* Signs of children becoming perfectionistic are as follow:

1.   They are afraid to do the task.

2.   They avoid the task.

3.   They cry or are defensive if scolded during the task.

4.   They get upset if little details are out of order, no matter how silly details seem to you.

5.   Their temper flares quickly.

6.   They promptly point out mistakes other kids make.

7.   They are very self-critical.

8.   They have very short attention spans, especially if task seems difficult.

9.   They have difficulty accepting compliments or complimenting themselves. Any exceptional behavior is considered normal. The more exceptional it is, the more embarrassed they are hearing others praise them.

10. They may do ritualistic or obsessive–compulsive actions.

What are *ritualistic or obsessive–compulsive actions?* Not a pretty sight, believe me. Ritualistic actions are when your child does a series of behaviors in exactly the same or near–same sequence when under pressure or showing signs of stress. One child, for instance, went through a whole routine before going to bed at night. First he turned his light off, then pulled his blanket half way down his bed, then checked his closet to make sure all the hangers were lined up the same way, and then he took only 4 steps (no more than 4) to get into bed. Every night he followed the same routine fearing that deviation from it might upset *something*, but he didn't know what.

Obsessive–compulsions are more severe. Imagine the same scenario with more intensity. That same child anticipates bedtime and the ritual he must go through before going to sleep. The more he worries, the more anxious he feels. This is the *obsessive* part. Anxiety initially dissipates when he *executes the behavior that he is compelled to do*. As if his repeating thoughts drove him to begin the ritual. Anxiety finally disappears when the entire ritual is over. Now he can relax and his worries vanish.

Toughing out ritualistic and obsessive–compulsive behavior can be hair–pulling. Parents witnessing this for the first time are shocked. "Such a small thing to get upset about?" Your perplexity may accidentally trip you into mistakes on dealing with this behavior. So, here are some "no–no's" on handling perfectionism:

DON'T:

1.   Yell at your child. (That only worsens his fear of mistakes.)

2.   Force corrections for mistakes. (That only confirms how bad a mistake is and the need to correct it every time.)

3.   Criticize your child for being too sensitive. (All he hears is criticism and then associates it with the mistakes being made or that could be made.)

4.   Talk to other children, siblings or adults about his or her perfectionism in listening distance to your child . (That also confirms the seriousness of his or her problem.)

5. Sympathize with your child's worries or sensitivity to mistakes. (This seems rude, but sympathy only draws attention to his superstitious fears about errors.)

Mistakes parents make in part are normal and cannot be helped. The hardest mistake is failing to realize that you may, yourself, be perfectionistic and doing exactly the same behaviors you despise in your child. Be aware of your intense impact as a persuasive model upon your child. He watches you, how you speak, act and react with uninterrupting interest.

Besides yourself, others in your family may also be perfectionistic and having an influence upon your child. Try to spot who it is and talk with that person about their behavior, that it is contagious, and the need for monitoring it around your child. At worst, that adult may deny being perfectionistic and think you're crazy. At best, that adult may sympathize with your concerns and make extra efforts at loosening up. On the homefront, here is what you can do if your child is perfectionistic:

DO THESE THINGS:

1.   Have your child say "It's No Big Deal or NBD" when getting upset.

2.   Make sure you keep your child in the situation when he gets upset. Refuse to allow your child to avoid more of the task or escape the task entirely. Keep your child hammering away at the task despite his protestations. For instance, if she crumbles up a paper after misspelling her name on it, insist she unravel the paper and continue using it. Refuse to let her get a new sheet of paper to start over.

3.   When your child is self–critical, wait a minute or two (do not respond immediately, lest you draw too much attention to the inappropriate behavior). Then ask your child to compliment himself on some aspect of the task. It can be anything, from how careful the work is, to how well your child understands the task. Be sure compliments pertain to real (not made up) aspects of the task. For instance, encourage your child to say, "I do a great job at drawing lines," or "math is really easy for me."

4.   Have your child speak positively or boastfully to somebody else about a recent accomplishment. Expect this to be difficult for your child. So, make it a short statement. You may even have to spoon feed the statement to your child, such as "Jenny, tell Uncle Jerry what nice thing your teacher said to you in modeling class." Jenny may refuse, may be shy, turn red all over in embarrassment or withdraw by walking or running away. Without too much hassle, retrieve her back to the scene and repeat your request. At least get Jenny to make some positive remarks about herself.

5.   Contrive situations for your child to make mistakes. This seems cruel at first. Here your child is phobic about mistakes and all you can do is stick his face in it. But actually confrontation with the phobia leads to fast relief of anxiety and perfectionism. Here's how you do it. Ask your child to try a task that you deliberately set up to be difficult. Mistakes *will happen in one form or another*. Tell your child ahead of time that any mistakes made are okay. That if your child feels afraid he is to say "It's No Big Deal (NBD)" and continue on with the task. Do not start over. Length of tasks vary but should remain under 15 minutes.

When your child works through the 15–minute task without delay for 3 days in a row, increase the length to 30 minutes. Increase time length by 15 minutes each time there are 3 days in a row without a snag.

6.   Make a distinct point to make mistakes yourself in front of your child. Silly as this seems, it makes a difference. Spill something, drop something, cut something wrong, or do any error in close proximity, followed by saying "its No Big Deal."

The hardest chore in stopping perfectionism is catching it when it occurs. So much of fear behavior is *private.*, that is, in the form of thinking or feelings, which are out of visual reach. Look for it on the surface and apply these tactics every chance you get.

When These Steps Are Working
Okay, so now you know side–effects of not following instructions and quick ways to handle them. That's nice. But what about signs of progress? How do you know when your child really is doing a

great job? Obvious answer, isn't it? When she follows instructions the way you want your child to. That makes good sense, doesn't it? Yes, it does. But that's only part of progress. How well your child hurries to finish a chore only means your tactics are effective. What about the next step beyond just following instructions? The step where children follow instructions so well and so consistently that you can't remember the day when they never listened to you.

That day does come. It happens when children are so used to hearing instructions that they begin to copy the format you use and now they use it back on you. Except you may not like the Frankenstein you created. "I wanted her to mind me, not manipulate me!" Let's see what this means.

Your Child asks the "If–Then." (Bossy Children)

Finally your child minds you. Instead of repeating instructions twice, three times, even four times, all you have to do is say it politely the first time with an"if–then" clause, and poof! Instruction followed within seconds. It all seems too easy. A dream come true. And then one day your sweet, lovable child pulls a royal stunt on you that deflates this miracle. He walks up to you in an unsuspecting manner and chants, "Dad, if I take out the garbage, will you let me stay up to watch a movie on HBO?"

"Did I hear that correctly?" You're stunned. Shocked. And sweat starts inching down your forehead as you try to keep calm. But you feel anger. Anger is on its way through your spine and at any moment will blast out in your voice. Your thoughts keep spinning. Only one thought stands out: "That bossy child! Who does he think he is?"

Let me tell you who he thinks he is. Your child is superb. Trying to bargain with you using those "if—then" statements like you did does not mean your child is bossy. Hardly so. Use of "if–then" statements reflects your child's *internalized understanding of rules and ability to be productive.* Meaning, it is an excellent signal that your child is in advanced stages of following instructions and that it has become a natural part of his personality.

When you hear your child make these statements,
DO NOT:
1. Criticize your child for being bossy, for undermining your authority, for trying to play

parent, or for pushing your buttons. (Because none of these are true.)

2.   Criticize your child for bad negotiating, for being selfish or lacking respect (again, not true).

3.   Criticize your child for being manipulative.

INSTEAD, DO THIS:

1.   Listen to what your child has to say.

2.   Discuss her "If–Then" clause and work it out so that you can comply to a request providing it sounds sensible.

3.   Compliment your child for taking initiative using this "if–then"clause. Make your child feel responsible and good for being more adult–like.

4.   Encourage your child to use this format around his or her friends or even around some (not all) adults. (Some adults, unsympathetic to your cause, may sabotage good behavior by insisting that the "If–Then" is grossly disrespectful. Be alert to this and do not believe their opinions as confirmation of your own wrong belief.)

Rules start for self–control (Self–Control)

Children braving the "If–Then" clause are on the their way up the road to success. Sounds presumptuous, you say? That all they are doing is copying what adults say to them? Being a parrot with words and phrases but not really grasping the meaning behind it? Well, that may be true for 0 to 2 year olds. But three years and older who speak fluently and carry on an intelligible conversation can use the "If–Then" clause *and really mean what they say and say what they mean.*

This is because the "If–Then" clause is a primary step to having self–control. It doesn't happen rapidly but changes in how your child sees himself and the world make self–control possible. Here's how it all takes place.

From "If–Then" to Self–Control

Did you know that things your child hears aloud or says to himself aloud eventually become what your child thinks? It's true. Words, phrases, or descriptions of action first spoken in daily conversation are converted into words, phrases or descriptions of actions your child thinks about when alone. This happens for everything he hears. Compliments spoken aloud to children are compliments they repeat to themselves in private, as thoughts. Bad things told to your children, unfortunately, follow the same pattern. Everything children hear or talk about makes up the substance of their thinking.

Knowing this, it's easier to follow the path from what children hear through development of self–control. This is the order it takes:

1.   *First*, your child hears you say "if you do this, then I'll do this." Your child hears that many times. The more you follow through accurately with this "If–Then" promise, the more your child believes these words are true.

2.   *Second*, your child copies your "If–Then" clause aloud. She tries it out with you, with friends, with other adults, and with strangers. Success with the "If–Then" clause increases your child using it. Failure with the "If–Then" clause stops future attempts to use it.

3.   *Third,* your child hears himself using this clause so many times that now it becomes second-nature. Children think about the phrase before saying it, after saying it, or may plan on variations of the phrase for different people. It becomes a popular thought.

4.   *Fourth,* your child starts to use this effective "If–Then" clause on himself. The "If" step turns into "If I do this..." And the "Then" step turns into "Then I can do this." No longer is anybody else needed in the "If–Then" sequence since your child can do it all alone. He may approach you and say, "Mom, I'm going to clean my room and then go out to my friend's house." It's no longer a question ("May I do this?"). Your child firmly states an "If–Then" that applies to only your child and does not require your approval. A very independent step.

5.   *Fifth,* verbally stated "Ifs and Thens" fade out and are replaced by your child just *doing the things in right order.* Your child now automatically *does the task or responsibility first, followed by the fun or rewarding activity.* If asked what he is doing, your child will reply in a matter–of –fact way that a reward follows a task. Just like telling you what

time their favorite TV show is on or what clothing is cool or popular in school. No hesitation, no dwelling on maybe this or maybe that—right to the point like a fact known for centuries.

6.   *Sixth,* your child takes on the role of expert. He may not be perfectionistic, but will point out when you and other people do not follow through on promises.

7.   *Seventh,* your child appears extremely organized, tasks put into a time schedule or following a rational order. Your child may even be an organizer for other people, or gladly accept adult responsibility from mom and dad on planning activities or making decisions.

One way or another, evolving rules on how to do things punctually and efficiently turn your child into a very independent person. It all started from your consistent use of "Ifs and Thens" and mushroomed to amazing heights of self–control. Children who do internalize these "If–Then" clauses or "rules" are well on their way to becoming ambitious, productive and highly successful career-minded adults.

CHAPTER 6

Controlling Your Anger

"Control your anger!" Ever heard someone say that to you? Probably. And you hated it. Anybody would. Nobody likes to be criticized and especially hearing that you are out of control. But let's face it. Calming down in tense situations is tough to do. When things aren't going right you get upset, and possibly lose your cool. Losing your cool around children is even more common.

Every parent knows it is impossible to be perfectly composed over every mishap in the household. Nobody can just "turn the other cheek" and pretend the antique dish didn't break, or pretend the milk really didn't spill all over your typed papers for school. Forget it. These things really happen. And the sooner reality hits you, the stronger you are against your anger.

This chapter is a special one. It talks about what actually makes parents angry above and beyond their child's behavior. Parts of anger called "urges" are laid out for you to spot, stop, and surrender before body tension escalates into raging aggression. First, let's get an idea of what causes an urge, and then spend the rest of the chapter focusing on simple ways to control your urge.

What is an Urge?

Urges are stressful periods of life usually lasting a short while but hectic to deal with. Urges can be a powerful drive to want something, or get away from something, or making something happen. Motivation to speak, act or react is strong or *urgent*. Urges are not automatic. They are caused by six things that happen at any given moment. These include:

1.   **You are under a time limit.**
2.   **You want something.**
3.   **There are no alternatives to choose from.**
4.   **You have two or more things you want to do simultaneously.**

5.   You have obstacles in the way of doing something.
6.   In the past you had bad experiences with situations like these.

1.   You are under a time limit.

Rushing around a busy household and balancing the juggling act of kids, office and leisure can be a mess. Routines get interrupted, delayed or modified. Something always goes wrong. No matter how early you awoke that morning, or told the kids time and again to be ready for school, it always happens. They forget. You forget. And the best laid plans of mice and men evaporate into thin air.

The balancing act gets more difficult when there is a time pressure. You *must* get to work on time. Kids *must* be outside for the school bus.You *must* get to the doctor's appointment by the hour. And the list abounds with countless reasons that time suddenly becomes a scarce commodity. When this happens, limits on time spoil patience. Time deadlines mobilize you into a frenzy of actions, from speeding up your pace to forcing others around you to rush. Perhaps you can do it. But generally kids cannot. The faster they go, the more mistakes they make; they more confused they get; the

more tired they feel; and the more angrier they become.

2. *You want something.*

You want it when? Right now—anytime or
anyway, that's how parents frequently feel under
the pressure of wanting something very specific.
How they get it really is less important than obtaining it in the first place.

Needs that you have range from biological
urges such as hunger or thirst to personal needs
such as having private time or watching television.
At times the desire for needs is higher than other
times. Under physical pain or fatigue, laying down
to take a nap is highly desirable. Hunger from
missing breakfast and lunch causes intense cravings
for food.

Or maybe the situation dictates immediate
action. A fly is still on the wall and in perfect target
range for the fly swatter, but must be hit within
seconds or else it flies away.

Fulfillment of needs may be important, but it
compromises your child's needs and interferes with
logical, concrete reasoning. Take, for example,
when Jacob, Andy's father, stopped in the middle of
helping Andy with his homework to catch a

mosquito. Naturally mosquitos pose *some* danger to his son, but *not that much danger*. Jacob climbed up on top of a weakly supported chair to block the mosquito in its path and made futile swats that put spots on the wall.

Jacob's *compulsive* need to divert attention to the mosquito shows he has little tolerance to wait until later or at least until after helping Andy with his homework. The faster urges are acted upon, the more aggressively explosive an adult's behavior will appear.

3.   *There are no alternatives to choose from.*

Urges also arise when decisions about some task are elusive. You are up against a mountain of problems all pointing in one direction that is unpleasant. Alternatives simply are out of touch or impossible.

Making sandwiches seems simple enough, for instance, but what if there is no bread, no meat, no cheese, and other substitutes are gone? Frustration rises little by little, mounting into agitation the more you realize there are no alternatives immediately available to make the kids sandwiches. Does that mean they go hungry? That's the unpleasant conclusion. Other solutions might be fingertips away but are not thought about at the time.

4.   *You have two or more things you want to do simultaneously.*

Plans always backfire to some extent but how much disruption you experience is never entirely predictable. That's the case with doing things simultaneously. No doubt you are one of those talented, ambidextrous parents able to listen to 3 conversations simultaneously while washing dishes, or typing a letter. It's an art and requires acute attention to the tasks at hand while ignoring thousands of distractions.

Most people can do two to three tasks simultaneously, usually talking on the phone while busy with some other errand. Concentration remains strong, until miniature voices creep out of the woodwork asking you questions or demanding attention. Interruptions of one task is annoying, but interrupting two, three or multiple ongoing tasks creates momentary panic, disorientation, and usually the flack is taken out on children.

5.   *You have obstacles in the way of doing something.*

Many situations arise where you know exactly what you want to do but cannot do it because of obstacles. Driving to work this morning, perhaps you let out a scream at the terrible traffic from road construction. Construction that started early that morning and you knew nothing about. It delays you from work, from running errands, and from going about your business. Still, unplanned obstacles also have the nasty side–effect of causing urges. You are stuck; a victim trapped by unavoidable and inescapable roadblocks that threaten your efficiency. Obstacles in the way of your life may sabotage plans but they also eat away at patience around childrens' behavior.

6.   *In the past you had bad experiences with sitpreadolescenceuations like these.*

Not every situation is bad. In fact, even unpleasant events in your past history undergo changes through years of experience. However, there are situations that stay the same no matter how many different approaches you try or tell yourself, "c'mon, it's not that bad." When, in fact, it really is bad. It's bad because somewhere lying in your archive of experiences you had a nasty encounter with certain people, objects or events associated with the situation.

Beth's mother, for example, hates stopping along the road at antique shops. Beth enjoys it, but her mother hates it with a passion. Together with another friend, Beth talked her mother into visiting a country antique store off the highway just for a few minutes. A few minutes was all it took. The moment Beth's mother stepped inside the store her face grimaced, tension flared, and she was eager to leave the store. Fearful situations take a toll on patience and make you more anxious around a child's misbehavior.

Another example of "bad associations" with a place is where your child had temper tantrums. Grocery stores are classic tantrum locations. It almost seems like all the children in the block conspire every Saturday morning to act out violently in local grocery stores. But of course that's not true.

Grocery stores, like any store, are open season for children's attention–seeking reactions because you react so quickly to the behavior. In less open spaces or where embarrassment is minimal, quick–draw reactions also are minimal. Grocery stores, clothing stores, malls, and restaurants all may hold pleasant memories for you—before children.

But because your child's misbehavior was uncontrollable in these locations you now avoid these like the plague unless you travel there alone. If, for any reason, solitary travel is impossible or by accident you visit a mall *and then remember why you hate going there,* tensions felt cause you to be impatient.

These five conditions make urges occur. Surprisingly, most people are unaware urges strike when they are feeling stressful or off guard. Or, that urges always follow a predictable pattern from start to finish.

Pattern of Urges

Urges go through very distinct steps as they slowly develop and become hectic. Finally they are out of control. Lack of control is nothing to be proud of but neither should you be ashamed of uncontrolled urges. Everybody experiences them. Watch out for urges as they rise in three steps: Threshold, Peak and Calm.

Threshold. Urges intensify more and more as time passes. At first a basic need, craving, or desire to do something remains harmless. Two minutes later that same harmless urge is eating away like a cancer at your conscious. Why is this?

The threshold stage describes a period when two predictable changes happen inside of you that are not visible to other people. Quickly, as if propelled by a cannon, you feel physical changes, followed by changes in thinking.

Physical changes appear in the autonomic or involuntary nervous system that controls respiration, circulation, digestion, glands and other reflexes. Sudden increases occur in heart beat, pulse rate, swallowing, blinking, sweating, and muscle contractions around the stomach, chest, shoulder and neck.

Muscle tension also feels like a "butterfly taking flight" in your stomach mixed with flush sensations rushing up and down your spine. Face color may change, and hands become wet with perspiration. Your stimulated nervous system charges a rush of adrenalin creating more and more discomfort.

Physical arousal is similar to food, alcohol or drug withdrawal. At first slowly building tensions graduate to desperate needs. You feel your body aching for the thing, object or event you want and delaying its attainment shortens your patience. Five to ten minutes into an urge episode the autonomic effects may worsen to watery eyes, stomach cramps, pacing, and need for urination.

Right in the heat of autonomic arousal your thoughts spring forth with ideas that *something is very wrong.* You recall in Chapter 3 about never taking personally a child's behavior; well, here's the real test.

Muscular stiffness paired with your insides doing acrobatics *will automatically trigger thoughts about doom, anger and blame.* Hard to control are vicious thoughts regarding why you *must* do the thing you want and *why it has no business being delayed.* Thoughts shout out to you in echoing thunder seemingly heard by everybody standing around you. But not so; only you hear them. Bursting thoughts usually take one of these themes:

1. Where is the thing?
2. Why isn't it here now?
3. What's wrong with the person who was supposed to bring it to me?
4. Things like this always happen to me!
5. This delay is inexcusable!

Thinking statements flow in and out obsessively with anger directed either at yourself for *be-*

ing so stupid, or at another person for depriving you of the need you want. Hank waited and waited for his son to finish in the bathroom. Eight year old Billy just didn't move that quickly. The drive to school took 10 minutes and school started in 15 minutes, leaving little leeway time in between. Hank initially was calm and asked Billy to hurry up.

Three to four minutes passed before Hank's rough voice escalated to a startle of "let's move it, Billy." Still, nobody exits the bathroom. Pacing around after 8 minutes was just about all Hank could stand for. "Hey, let's do an abbreviated version, shall we!"

Angry thoughts infecting Hank's mind all revolved around his urge to leave for school. He *had to be there on time*. But obstacles arose. Time pressures were interrupted by unplanned toileting needs of his son, and then Billy *took his time in the bathroom*, or so Hank thought. Stress elevated to this point builds on the input of irrational, illogical and simply wrong thinking about why Billy caused this inconvenience to Hank.

Disturbed thinking diverts attention from the real situation and leads to attacks upon the innocent scapegoat child. It does damage to the afflicted child for he cannot understand what he did wrong.

Billy, like most children, scares easily. He trembles and stiffens at the shrieking voice of his father's anger, believing that he is bad or has somehow disappointed in his father. He is *ashamed*. In other words, one deadly result of parents uncontrolled urges at the threshold stage is forcing guilt upon their children and rendering them afraid, reluctant, and passive.

Peak. This stage marks the natural turning point of urges. As time increases, intensity of urges also increases, reaching the peak at the very top.

Now your anger is really rolling. By the peak stage autonomic arousal is fully operational; muscle twitches and tightness are harder to hide. Visible anger permeates your entire body even if you are generally a mild–mannered person.

Friends and family looking at you might even ask if you are okay or suffering an illness. They're not accustomed to seeing this behavior in you—nor are you. Behaviors you display shift from anger to sadness to manic and bizarre explosions of frustration.

Mood swings also are heavily verbal and physical. You swear, become defensive, and yell. It seizes the child's vulnerability; you paralyze the child's emotions when verbal assaults turn to violent physical actions. Throwing papers, chairs, threats, even stumping up and down or hurting objects or people nearby—all result from not getting what you want when you want it.

It sounds "childish," but the behavior is quite adultlike. Resounding temper tantrums set off by urges and worsened by delaying gratification is what anger is all about. By the time anger defuses and the wave passes, damage done to all who watched you is unforgivable and largely irreversible.

The Calm after the Storm. Scientifically, urges pass through both threshold and peak before they subside. Twenty to thirty minutes after urges first start, with no relief still in sight, parents take on a new attitude about the urge; "oh well." They surrender to the urge in their own defeated attempts to get what they wanted without any luck. Surrender, however, is not always a passively helpless experience.

There are two ways parents resign to defeat. First is openly admitting failure but not seeking alternatives. Second is resisting failure and blaming oneself or your child for rudely depriving you of what you wanted. Let's consider these more closely.

Two Wrong Ways that parents react when urges fade

1.   ADMIT FAILURE BUT NOT SEEK NEW
      ALTERNATIVES

2.   RESIST FAILURE AND BLAME YOU OR
      YOUR CHILD

Admit failure and not seek new alternatives. You didn't get what you wanted or it took so long getting it that by now it really doesn't matter anymore. Parents may stop being angry, stop their assaults and desperate 11th hour attempts at being satisfied.

Now they turn to another way of solving the basic problem: How can I get what I want? Sally's mother, Sharon, really wanted to pick up a few groceries at lunch before returning to work. Except she also had to shuttle Sally from elementary school to her dance lesson starting at 1:00. By the time Sharon snuck out of the office and made it to her car, less than a half hour was left to pull off her Houdini stunt.

She arrived at Sally's school in minutes. Then proceeded to the grocery store. *Forget it!* Traffic was too congested to pull off this trick. No matter how blatantly upset Sharon was toward other motorists for *being so stupid on the road,* time passed too quickly. She simply couldn't go to both places.

Sharon surrendered to time constraints and her anger vanished. But not before Sally took the brunt of her mother's anger. Anger is gone; no apologies, no solutions found. It just dies. And supposedly, everybody who suffered through the ordeal just forgets about it.

2. *Resist Failure and Blame You or Your Child.* The scenario could have been different. What if Sharon didn't let go of the anger? What if she took it out on herself or her daughter? Sharon's unmet urge might vanish due to passage of time, but her anger about not satisfying it lingers on.

Her distorted thinking becomes accusatory: she stews over why she *should have been able to do it,* and that her mistakes were *preventable.* Anguish over mistakes and failures triggers fierce self–

criticism, where Sharon finds herself *guilty, stupid and sloppy* for not satisfying her urges. She becomes judge and jury on proclaiming an unforgivable sentence of shame upon herself and all of her actions.

Self–imposed shame in front of small Sally is deadly. Impressionable Sally hears her mother rant and rave over trivial matters and is perplexed. Sally innocently wonders "why is she angry?" It doesn't make sense? Over small, insignificant obstacles? Or is anger for special occasions? Should parents reserve a tirade for earth–shaking catastrophes affecting your personal life and family? If Sally picks the first one, angry over simple losses, her temper tantrums copy her mother's behavior in the natural flow of learning .

More scheming and dangerous, however, is when Sharon's agitation is expelled on her daughter. Being "fit to be tied, " Sharon may lay blame on Sally for any number of mishaps believed to sabotage the plan. "You were late getting outside; a couple of minutes earlier and I surely would have made it to the grocery store. Can't you do anything right?"

Indictments of flaws relieve Sharon from feeling guilty and self–critical. Somebody else becomes the target. Scapegoat Sally, vulnerable and incapable of rational recourse, is plotted against by being forced to absorb her mother's failures.

Sally's sinking pride already took a dive once when her mother started the tirade. That shocked and paralyzed Sally. Now her pride plummets deeper to the bottom of her gut. She is overwhelmed by shame for nothing she did wrong or even understands.

Is there any way that Sharon, like other mothers and fathers can prevent angry outbursts and the awful side–effects it has for children? Yes. there is. Overcoming urges and anger is a simple process and almost too easy to be true. Nobody said controlling anger had to be difficult. And it isn't.

Controlling Your Anger and Urges

Urges are deadly weapons against patience. Just saying to yourself, "c'mon, calm down" is just too weak to stop anger. Common sense reminders only sound good but never restore tranquility, until after the fact. Later that day or evening it is easier to rehearse through what you *could have done or should have done.* Let us walk through different strategies that go beyond common sense for better urge control. First is the *Stop–Look–Lower* approach. Second is calming down your body with easy–to–use relaxation steps.

People give advice that ignoring your urges will make them go away. Sounds great. But what happens? It doesn't go away. In fact, urges never go away. They only fade in and out of the scenery with different intensity. Urges recur because there are other factors going on that must be considered at the time. That is what this section does. Let's consider some other factors affecting urges, starting with the *Stop–Look–Lower* approach.

Stop–Look–Lower

Anger follows along the time sequence of threshold and then peak until it finally cools down. You can prevent or interrupt your anger by looking carefully at events going on and what can be done to rearrange them. That is what *Stop* is all about. "Stop" right in your tracks as you feel muscular tension and flush sensations flowing up and down your spine. Look around at exactly where you are, what is going on, and time schedules. Ask these questions:

1.   Am I under a time limit?

2.   Am I at a loss for options?

3.   Am I upset because I think I can't do this?

4.   Is what I want to do being interrupted?

5.   Do I want something I can't get?

6.   Am I doing two things simultaneously?

7.   Are there too many obstacles in the way?

8.   Am I reading too much into this unpleasant situation?

Answers of "yes" to each item mean urges exist and are disrupting your concentration, especially around children. The next step after realizing your difficulty, is to *look*; around for ways to change these limiting conditions and free yourself of urge traps.

For instance, is there any way of giving yourself more time? Or dropping the compulsive need for something which also eliminates the need to negotiate with its obstacles. You can gain a new lease on life simply by forcing yourself to rapidly identify as many ways as possible to remove the eight problems shown above.

Jackie's father, Bruce, felt his insides fuming over the spilled milk and he was on the verge of explosion when he *stopped* and *looked*. Here is what he quickly discovered:

1.   *Am I under a time limit?* Yes. I must leave for work within 5 minutes and drive Jackie to day-care first before driving in the snow another 5 miles to work.

2.   *Am I at a loss for options?* Yes. Darn milk spilled on my tie but I can't figure out another tie that matches with this outfit.

3.   *Am I upset because I think I can't do this?* Yes. Matching clothing is not my specialty. Usually I check out outfits with my wife the night before and now my wife is at work. Choosing this tie right now is something new for me.

4.   *Is what I want to do being interrupted?* Yes. That milk spilling delays us taking off with little time to spare.

5.   *Do I want something I can't get?* Yes. Ideally I'd like to be on the road heading to work in this lousy weather but the more I rush the farther behind I get at this goal.

6.   *Am I doing two things simultaneously?* Yes. I was reading the paper, correcting Jackie's homework, and carrying on a conversation with her. All together these activities probably overlooked her need for me to pour the milk in her cereal.

7.   *Are there too many obstacles in the way?* Yes. Choosing the tie creates obstacle number one of not knowing which tie. Cleaning the table is obstacle number two. And the lousy snowy weather is obstacle number three.

8.   *Am I reading too much into this unpleasant situation?* Yes. I assumed Jackie's spilled her milk for being in a hurry or because she was sloppy.

Alert to his mistakes, now Bruce can *lower* his anger by trying out new alternatives that change the complexion of these conditions. Changes he puts immediately into practice include the following:

1.   *Am I under a time limit?* Yes. And I can change this by calling up her daycare or my office and saying I'll be a bit late due to the weather and small accident with the spilled milk.

2.   *Am I at a loss for options?* Yes. But I can change this by creating new options such as asking Jackie to help clean up, while I change my tie.

3.   *Am I upset because I think I can't do this?* Yes. But I can change this by picking out a tie myself regardless of what people or my wife might think.

4.   *Is what I want to do being interrupted?* Yes. But I can change this by allowing for more time and expecting more interruptions along the way. Interruptions are accidental, not deliberate, and usually occur when doing new or foreign behaviors or are up against unexpected challenges such as the snowy weather.

5.   *Do I want something I can't get?* Yes. But I can change this by slowing my pace down and real-

izing more time is needed to get what I want in smaller steps.

6.   *Am I doing two things simultaneously?* Yes. I now need to do one task at a time. When I dabble in several tasks simultaneously I must stop for a moment, pay attention to what's going on, and then return to the task.

7.   *Are there too many obstacles in the way?* Yes. But each obstacle is only troublesome when I rush. Slowing down the pace allows for concentration and less errors.

8.   *Am I reading too much into this unpleasant situation?* Yes. I need to check out my facts by asking Jackie what happened, or putting two and two together including how I was at fault. Blaming Jackie only reverses my anger onto her and makes me feel momentarily better. Whereas ownership of at least some blame forces my awareness of the true facts and steps toward correction.

Relaxation

Popular remedies for relaxation crowd bookstore shelves. Is relaxation achieved through pure imagery? Will visualizing a beach scene in the middle of a department store while your son is screaming at the top of his lungs *really* soothe the spirit? Probably not. How about through acupuncture or medications? Will prescribed sedatives or tranquilizers calm your nerves when Samantha spits up her asparagus on your freshly cleaned floor? For a moment, maybe. But that's it. Medicine for urge control is a poor choice.

Parents who rely on medicines are kidding themselves. Fast–acting relaxants such as Valium®, Xanax®, Buspar®, Ativan®, among others, are for another purpose. Their compounds distinctly help lower severe anxiety attacks and out of control fears brought on by much more than unwanted stressors. Taking these pills slows your pace down all right, but it also causes side–effects such as drowsiness, disorientation, and sometimes interferes with coordination. Worst of all, relying on medicines as urge controllers gets you into the *habit*. One pill a day doesn't keep the doctor away—it brings you to the doctor more and more for prescription refills because you can't get along without the medicines. Dependency on pills is scary, especially when stressors get you all worked up and there are no pills around. What do you do?

You freak out, literally. Tolerance to medicines forces higher doses and frequent refills to keep you at a balanced state. If popping a pill is your habit under stress, absence of pills will put you in greater excitable fear and paralyze your coping mechanisms with acting out children. Withdrawal symptoms emotionally felt are anger, irritability, and intolerance. Add up these symptoms along with not knowing how to manage children and the sum total is more severe anxiety than you started off with before taking the medicine.

In other words, think twice, and three times before resorting to this solution for relaxation. A better start is focusing on your muscles. There are muscles that tense up or painfully hurt during urge episodes as you enter threshold and later peak stages. Painful muscular discomfort happens in different spots around your body and you can release this tension following basic steps no matter where you are. Steps include:

Step 1. Locate the Tension.

Step 2. Intensify and De–intensify.

Step 1. Locate the Tension

Where is it? Where is the tension coming from? This is the first step to relaxation. Most people say tension is felt in the back, neck, thighs, stomach, or wherever there is contact with furniture, clothing or activity. For instance, backache is tension from sitting all day in hard chairs. Foot pain comes from wearing small shoes. Eye strain from eye fatigue after staring all day at the jiggling black and white computer screen. And so forth.

But tension forms around more than one critical part of the body. Stiffness, muscle spasms or general discomfort can be described on three regions. The first region of muscles includes the head, face, forehead, eyes, mouth, cheekbones, and neck. The second or "middle" region covers the stomach, shoulders, arms, wrists and fingers. A third region includes thighs, legs, feet and toes.

Finding tension among these regions is simple. It doesn't require medical knowledge. Rather, look at yourself and verbally name each of the three muscle areas. At the sound of your voice, assign a number between "0" and "10" to show how much tension is felt. A "0" indicates no tension and "10" indicates much stiffness and tightness.

Now put yourself through a short test. Deliberately stay in tune with your body's muscles while watching, but not acting upon your child's disruptive behavior. Sit there for a moment during a tantrum episode or after he refuses to pick up his clothes. Say nothing for the moment. To yourself record the number (0 to 10) best describing the discomfort you feel. All "10's?" Identify exactly where the "10's" are located. In the first region, second region, or third region? What part of the body?

Frequent muscle restriction, for instance, happens in the first and second regions. In the first region are tight forehead, clenching your teeth, and tight back of neck. In the second region are tight chest, shoulder stiffness, and abdominal tightness. Feel discomfort in any one of these areas? If you do, move rapidly to step 2.

Step 2. Intensify and De–Intensify

Pressure build–up is usually a familiar sensation. Most parents know when their body feels in stitches. However, to tell the difference between tension and no tension, attention has to be paid to what muscles feel like when tension goes away. An exercise teaching this sensation to you involves the step of *intensify and de–intensify*.

Intensify is intentionally adding more tension to the known discomfort. It sounds funny, but is very true. Pile more pressure upon the constricted muscle zone by flexing it a bit. Added tension sends a clear message to your body on how hurtful pressure feels. Since sensations vary among muscles, intensifying also familiarizes you with how different muscle groups react under stress.

De–intensify is the favorite part. Release the tightness like a balloon popping. Just let go. All the pressure built up in the intensify part vanishes instantly. It's gone. De–intensify is eliminating pressure so that you can feel the naturally relaxing sensations for a moment or two. Let that free–flowing sensation continue until the muscle begins feeling prickly or "asleep," as when your foot falls asleep. Resist temptation to shake off that sensation or engage in motion to prevent it. As tingling sensations begin, let your hands gently rest on whatever objects are around you. If sitting, place your hands gently on the seat cushion. If standing, lay them gently by your side.

The sequence of intensify to de–intensify goes like this:

INTENSIFY MUSCLES——–>WAIT 3 to 5 seconds——–>DE–INTENSIFY MUSCLES

It's helpful to repeat the intensify and de–intensify steps twice on each muscle identified as feeling tight. In fact, practice this exercise at first in private. In bed before getting up in the morning, try out these steps by tightening and loosening problem muscles in each of the three regions. Verbally say to yourself, "tighten, hold, and now loosen."

Effectively using this technique every time urges arise can block that urge from shifting into second and third gear up the ladder to threshold and peak. Control is possible, in other words, but it depends on your deliberate energy to try it out. And that's only the beginning.

Parents who use relaxation agree there is one problem with it. Will I always have time to use it? They think intensify and de–intensify steps take great time and labor involving laying down, working through every muscle, and achieving perfect karma. Well, not so. It's hard enough stealing a free moment of personal time away from child rearing, let alone a half hour or so for relaxation. That's why relaxation does not require removal of the stressor. *Don't leave the hectic situation. Stay right there.* Use relaxation steps as you feel pressure building directly in the middle of coping with problems. Here is how relaxation fits in these different places.

At home. Miserably rising anger can be countered by stop–look–lower method plus sitting down in a chair or couch. Go through each of the pressured muscles until the tension is gone. Then re–enter the situation using proper methods to handle the situation.

At stores. Rising anger can be countered first, by locating a less busy spot in the store. If using a shopping cart, lean on it with your hands and arms and go through relaxation steps. Next, loosen other bothersome muscular regions before moving the cart. Move the cart forward only when you are ready to press onward. If there is no place to "hide," go into an aisle, pick up a product from the shelf, and concentrate on it while leaning on the cart and undergoing relaxation steps.

At grandma/grandpa's home. This is tougher. There's no doubt about it. At least in stores you can remain anonymous. Here, the audience knows who you are, and what's bothering you. If it is your parents' home, treat it like your own home by locating a chair or couch and begin the exercises. Refuse to explain or defend your actions during relaxation despite persistent inquiries from your parents. And believe me, they will inquire feverishly.

Once basic muscles are calmer, return to the difficult situation.

At relatives' homes. Apologies seem greater when the stakes are higher. Here the people are close, but not close enough to be ignored. Again locate that chair or couch, and then ask if one of the adults (or spouse) can watch the misbehaving child for a few minutes. After muscular relief, return to the situation.

At friends' homes. Oddly, risk–taking is easier here because friends probably already know your struggles, fears, and new approaches. Repeat the same approach as if at a relatives house. Ask your friend to baby–sit for a couple of minutes while you seek refuge on a coach or chair and intensify, then de–intensify muscles.

At a restaurant. Humiliation was meant for restaurants. If another adult is at the table, physically remove the troublemaker (gently) to the lobby, private area, or outside to the car, weather permitting. If child is same gender as you, remove yourself and child to the bathroom. Once there, let child just wander a moment while you loosen discomfort and regain control over urges. This is about the only place where leaving the situation for a moment is appropriate. It's obvious why. Certainly your embarrassment is greater, but more problematic is the disruption caused to other people who came to the restaurant for a peaceful meal.

At daycare or school. Just the opposite is true here. Exposure of your child's misbehavior in school is perfectly normal while you calm yourself down. She is around a teacher, peers, and environment that sees the child every day. And hardly every day is a happy day. Again, ask the teacher to watch your son or daughter for a moment while you regain strength through relaxation. Then re–enter the situation.

At scouts, brownies or peer activities. Much like at daycare or school, your child is around peers and other adults. Rising urges can be subdued by excusing yourself for a moment, while your child stays with another adult. Locate that infamous chair or couch and restore muscular comfort.

Anger is Not Control

Anger is not control. Please don't confuse these. Because it's easy to think one means the other. Deterioration of patience may turn into anger as a way of cooling down the situation. It may work. In fact, yelling, screaming, even hitting seems effective because urges immediately disappear once behavior is under control. But just because behavior comes under control, does not mean that what controlled behavior was *anger*. It wasn't. It was fear.

Urges accelerate adult tempers in ways most parents keep silent. Nobody is proud of losing patience or disgracefully having a shouting match with their children. It feels wrong. Parents see their children being afraid, staying away from them or talking back even more in defiance of adult tempers. Yet, are adult tempers all that bad?

When anger accidentally leaks out of the emotional bucket it is not immediate cause for alarm. Mistakes do happen and parenting mistakes are even more inevitable. Anger is normal, as is feeling afraid or unhappy. Overly monitoring your actions to prevent any and all anger is futile. It slips out regardless of the best intentions because urges strike at odd times and are not always preventable and controllable. Last time you suffered the flu was a good example. Hard as you tried to remain sweet and fluffy, physical wear and tear on your body increased your sensitivity. Mildly loud sounds triggered a headache and rang in your eyes for days. Effort of any sort seemed like an endless mountain climb. And nothing, no matter how efficient your days were, seemed to go right. Illness destroys adult patience and makes you a moving target for uncontrolled urges. So, realize coping with child behavior means risking a burst here or there without it feeling like the end of the world.

Side–Effects of Too Much Anger

When anger is more than here and there, more than once in a while, that's when red–lights flash "warning signs." Frequent angry outbursts signal you are out of control and using your anger entirely for behavior manipulation. Why do you do this? Anger probably scares you as much as it scares the children watching you. But consciously or not, relying on anger in the form of punishment occurs for specific reasons. Consider if these reasons fit your own situation:

Do you use punishment :

1.   TO increase appropriate behavior?
2.   TO decrease inappropriate behavior?
3.   TO prevent anticipated inappropriate behavior?
4.   TO establish compliance?
5.   TO establish authority in themselves?
6.   TO establish trust in themselves?
7.   TO establish love?

Answers of "yes" to these questions suggest your urgency for control is strong. The bad news is that persistent anger and punishment backfire with miserable results. Punishment will not work in the long run and actually cause serious side–effects in behavior in the shortrun. Children exposed to recurrent and heavy punishment learn bizarre patterns typically described as:

1.   *Child learns to seek punishment for attention*. This means attention–seeking efforts (tantrums, defiance, etc.) entirely focus on drawing anger from parents.

2.   *Child pairs or associates properties of punishment with the person administering the punishment*. Children pair people with good things and bad things. Candies and ice cream paired with grandma and grandpa guarantees your child will perceive grandma and grandpa in a highly positive light. But the same pairing is possible for bad things. Hitting, yelling, screaming, and threats pair more rapidly with the person. This guarantees your child will perceive you as a bad, wicked and scary person.

3.   *Child avoids or gets out of (escapes) antici-pated or actual punishment situations.* Child vic-tims of frequent punishment quickly learn to stay clear of conflicts with parents and even if they anticipate conflicts may arise. No chances are taken. If caught off guard in the middle of conflict, quick thinking and execution of fear usually gets them out of the situation. They simply will not stay around for the torture. If forced to remain in place, sudden immobility takes over. Children literally learn to "freeze" still in one spot, not moving, not saying anything. They tremble inside with intense fear for their lives.

4.   *Child stops appropriate behavior for fear of punishment.* Even appropriate play and good behavior is interrupted once there is fear of punishment. Children just stop what they are doing, no matter how appropriate it is, and hide. This does damage to good behavior as much as bad behavior.

5.   *Child learns inappropriate behavior for avoidance and escape.* A serious risk is learning bizarre or inappropriate ways to secure avoidance and escape from fearful punishment. Children may

tell lies, feign illness, run away, steal, even consent to immoral or unethical behaviors (prostitution, pornography, etc.). Whatever it takes to prevent the fear.

6.   *Child never learns appropriate behaviors for peer group.* A child may run scared so much of the time that he never learns appropriate social skills. Avoidance and escape behaviors contaminate and monopolize the repertoire. There remains, then, little incentive to learn positive productive behaviors because they seem useless in life.

7.   *Child carries over avoidance and escape behavior to other situations.* Problem with avoidance and escape behavior is that it is not limited to one situation. It transfers all over the place from one situation to another situation even if punishment never occurred in the new situations. Transmission of behaviors from home to school is most common.

8.   *Child learns inappropriate reactions that interfere with not only normal behaviors but also the "opportunities" for normal learning.* Avoidance and escape further stifle risk–taking. Abused chil-

dren are squeamish about trying new toys, new friends, or exploring the unknown. They hesitate to seize opportunities fearing the shame and punishment of failure at them or being caught looking stupid. As these opportunities for growth pass them by, their peers mature ahead of them and may alienate the abused children.

9.   *Child learns to be immune or insensitive to adult authority.* Heavy doses of punishment also sterilize fear. Once children encounter fear again, and again, and again, it becomes second nature and they are immune to it. By age 8 or preadolescence, fear becomes so numbed that a child may say or do things showing no respect for authority. He no longer is conscious of right and wrong but instead acts on impulse, always avoiding or escaping conflict without regard for what other people think. This loss of shame or self–awareness indicates advanced stages of victimization and threatens to create the profile of a Charles Manson.

In Which House Does Your Child Live?

"I got two A's" the small boy cried.
His voice was filled with glee
His father bluntly asked,

"Why didn't you get three?"

"Mom, I've got the dishes done,"
the girl called from the door
Her mother very calmly said,
"Did you sweep the Kitchen floor ?"

"I've mowed the grass," the tall boy said,
"And put the mower away"
The father looking at his feet and rug said,
"Didn't you clean off the clay?"

The children in the house next door seem
happy and content.
The same things happen over there.
But this is how it went.

"I got two A's" the small boy cried,
His voice was filled with glee
His father proudly said "That's great!"
"I'm glad you belong to me."

"Mom, I've got the dishes done,"
the girl called from the door
Her mother smiled and softly said,
"Each day I love you more."

"I've mowed the grass," the tall boy said,
"And put the mower away"
His father answered with much joy,
"Son, you have made my day."

Source: *Author Unknown, Bay City Catholic Family Services
and Aegis, Midland County, Michigan.*

What Control Really IS

It's knowing. It's predicting. It's the defusal
of anger right when it starts and saying to yourself,
" Okay, what really is going on here?" Analyzing
the situation without assumptions and by sorting
through all the garbage can put you miles ahead of
your child in any situation. It's certainly a first step
using the *Stop–Look–Lower* method. Even better is
to *intensify and de–intensify* tight muscles before
they ruin your patience. But this still may not be
enough control over anger or over your child.

What will really help understand where
your child is coming from and ease your own desperation is *prediction*. Sounds funny, doesn't it?
"Prediction?" Your ability to use scientifically based
rules about behavior might save you much time,
effort and agony wondering your child's next

move. General "rules" tell what your child is likely to do given how you react to him or don't react to him. Will he respond kindly or unkindly after certain discipline—negative or positive? Will he terrorize you with tantrums or lie up and down until he turns blue in the face just to spite you? Answers to these questions make a difference.

For rules about behavior to mean something, they have to tie together how two people react. One person does one thing, and the other person responds to him. This is an *exchange*. Just as paying money for a dishwasher *in exchange* gets you the dishwasher, so acting toward your child in one way *in exchange* gets you a reaction from your child. Sometimes exchanges are rewarding—you smile and your child smiles back. Sometimes exchanges are punishing—you yell and your child yells back. And then the most peculiar of all situations. What if an exchange is both rewarding and punishing? How does your child react then?

If your curiosity is killing you, try out these three rules of exchanges. They are solid predictors of behavior to expect from your children when you behave a certain way first. Use them as guidelines. Note them: *reward exchanges, punishing exchanges*, and *simultaneous and delayed exchanges*.

Rewarding Exchanges:

1.   The more rewards given by a parent, the more amount of rewards returned by a child.

2.   **BUT,** the more rewards given for no reason (arbitrarily) by a parent, the less amount of rewards returned by a child.

3.   **AND,** the more reward given for clear reasons by a parent, the faster the rewards are returned by a child.

4.   The less amount of rewards given by a parent, the more amount of punishers (angry, defiance, tantrums, etc.) returned by a child.

5.   The more rewards are taken away after a parent gives them to a child, the faster the punishers are returned by that child.

6.   **AND,** if a parent gives rewards a lot, then stops giving them, the more a child demands substitutes or returns with punishers.

Punishing Exchanges:

1.   The more amount of punishers given by a parent, the less rewards returned by a child. And, the child will also give back more punishers to his parents. Where there has been many parental punishers, a child may avoid the exchange entirely.

2.   The more punishers given for no reason by a parent, the less punishers or rewards returned by a child. Where there has been many parental punishers, the child may avoid the exchange entirely.

3.   **AND,** the more punishers given for a reason by a parent, the more punishers returned by a child.

4.   **BUT,** the more punishers taken away after they are given by a parent, the more rewards returned by a child. This is to avoid future recurrence of punishers. (That is, child makes parent happy out of fear of being punished again, rather than out of love for that parent.)

5.   **LIKEWISE,** when punishers are absent, a child returns with rewards. This is also to avoid future recurrence of punishers.

Simultaneous and Delayed Exchanges:

1.   The more rewards and less punishers given by a parent simultaneously, the more punishers returned by a child.

2.   **AND,** the less rewards and more punishers given by a parent simultaneously, still the more punishers returned by a child.

3.   **EVEN** when equal amount of rewards and punishers are given by a parent simultaneously, the more that punishers are returned by a child.

4.   **EVEN** when rewards are given first, followed by punishers (within 30 minutes), still the more that punishers are returned by a child.

5.   **AND EVEN** when punishers are given first, followed by rewards (within 30 minutes), still the more that punishers are returned by a child. **OR,** a child will react with neither punisher nor reward.

The message is clear. Punishment fails. It nearly always is a turn off for your child no matter how quickly it stifles behavior. Punishers also leave a stronger impression; a lasting impression—but a bad one; a horribly negative impression. Consider this: Sweet talk your child with "I love you's," plus yummy hugs and kisses, followed by a rodeo show at the best circus in town. And if by mistake, right before he goes to sleep that evening, you lose your temper over something trivial, that anger wipes out every morsel of rewards for the whole day. That is how it is. Punishers always have and always will impose more fear and force upon children because children are fragile and lack skills to protect themselves.

Use the exchange rules as key reminders of how your child reacts to rewards and punishers. It may save you hours of saying to yourself, "Now, why did he do that?"

CHAPTER 7

Is There Life After Children?

Please tell me it's true. Otherwise, what happens to "my life" while children are growing up? Does it vanish into thin air? Does my life just stand still until the caretaking days are over? That's a dismal thought. Doing nothing until that day of liberation when the youngest child announces, "Okay, mom and dad, now it's your turn–thanks for sacrificing the last 20 years of your life for me." Right, like we're really going to wait until this happens. Fat chance.

And so many parents do not wait. This chapter looks at keeping yourself emotionally alive during child rearing years and particularly when there are snags along the way. Tantrums and noncompliance are bad enough snags. But imagine the additional grief from being a single parent, or divorced ("ex") parent, or starting over in a new "step" family. Does behavior get worse? Stay the same? Are there new strategies to get through these difficult times before they tear you apart? Sure there are. But let's take it one step at a time.

Married with Children

Not everybody is Al Bundy. Not everybody comes home after a slaving day ashamed of his family. *Married with Children*, the controversial Fox TV show, paints a comical but unrealistic picture of modern American households. Oh, there is a little apathy, greed, anger, and "leave me alone, I just want to breathe fresh air" in all of us. But parenting during marriage does not have to be all bad. In fact, plenty of happiness is possible following basic rules that allow time for yourself and your children. Consider how to do this by asking yourself:

1.   How do I see myself in the family?
2.   How can I make time for myself and my spouse?
3.   How can I make time for the kids?
4.   How do I let the kids become independent?

How Do I See Myself in the Family?

Playing "parent" seems a cruel game of self–denial if little or no time is devoted to yourself. The same is true for dealing with your family on a day to day basis. How do you do that? By pleading? Begging your kids to clean up? Or, by being the enforcer? Ordering your children and spouse to keep a prompt household schedule? Or do you play a different family role? There are seven roles most parents play in one way or another. Do any of these describe you?

1. therapy role
2. recreational role
3. sexual role
4. religious role
5. bystander role
6. enabler role
7. organizer role

Therapy role. Somebody has to patch emotional wounds and heal the bleeding mental hearts. Is it you? You can lose yourself if absorbed in working out all family conflicts. By the time you sort out who did what, why, and how they *feel about it*, they all walk away pleased as a pumpkin while you feel exhausted. It's too much to do alone. RESIST playing therapist, healer or problem–

solver for all family members. INSTEAD, make everyone share in the fact–finding, make–me–feel–good exercise.

Recreational role. So, where are we going today? The zoo? The park? Maybe out for pizza? Just the name the place and off we go. And there you go being activities director coordinating all the entertainment, sports, and family reunions until you turn blue in the face. It's a complex job. One that demands full commitment of time, energy, and insider awareness of what every family members loves. The problem is that while children and spouse are out and about, you're at home planning tomorrow's activities. Again, they win; you lose. RESIST believing you are the only one capable of planning family activities. INSTEAD, let each child—if old enough—and spouse volunteer ideas, make appointments, buy tickets and even juggle schedules so you can be happily as much a recipient as helper.

Sexual role. This is a tricky one. Ever feel that the only way of getting things done in the house or help with the kids is by having sex with your spouse. Your spouse never really spells this condition out for you, "Dear, if you do this, then I'll do this." Not exactly. But hints of this type broadcast the message loud and clear. Sexual favors initiated by yourself or spouse in return earn privileged assistance with child– rearing. RESIST buying into this vicious, addictive cycle by calling a spade a spade. INSTEAD, Let your spouse know child–rearing is not up for negotiation. It is a must. Both of you do it together just as you brought the child into life together.

Religious role. Who reminds the family when it's *wrong or immoral* to do something? Telling your children their actions were inappropriate seems normal–it is. But judging what is and is not normal takes on a religious or moral attitude that, by mistake, falls into your hands only. You become sole judge, jury and executioner. Your word is next to God. And you're kids resent you for it. Suddenly they identify you as the *mean* one. The other spouse in the meantime is their sounding board, calming their angry outbursts provoked by you, the mean authority figure. RESIST being the only person who dispenses moral, religious or ethical wisdom. INSTEAD, insist your spouse share this responsibility and apply discipline as frequently as you do.

Bystander role. Just sit back and watch the games commence. Do you ever take a spectator's role in family affairs? Going along with any and all decisions, orders, and needs expressed by the kids and spouse even if it really is not what you want to do? Playing the "bystander" role avoids problems such as conflict, angry child reactions, and stirring up misery that leaves you deeply stuck in guilt. RESIST passively surrendering to the whims of your family and being taken for granted. INSTEAD, be sure that all decisions, or as many as possible are mutual and reciprocal. Mutual means both you and your spouse acknowledge the value of the decision. Reciprocal means outcomes benefit you and your spouse whenever possible.

Enabler role. It is one thing to sit back and let the wind carry you away. It is another thing to plead with the wind until it takes you away. "Enabling" does this. Enablers go to great extremes to avoid, escape and prevent family duress at the expense of the enabler. Agreeing to sex for help with the kids, as said earlier, *enables* your spouse to satisfy selfish needs at your expense. Enabling always benefits another person as long as it minimizes your aggravation. The problem is that this aggravation you try desperately to extinguish has to be there in the first place for healthy families. Eliminating conflict and fears only feels good but does not keep things balanced. Just the opposite is true. Chaos occurs. Enabling people *always leads to*

1.   Spouse and kids getting what they want.
2.   Spouse and kids taking you for granted.
3.   Spouse and kids blaming you for not working hard enough.
4.   Spouse and kids treating you like a traitor.
5.   Spouse and kids verbally or even physically abusing you.
6.   Spouse and kids not listening to you when you finally put your foot down and demand changes.

RESIST avoiding family pressure by pleasing your spouse and children or by feeling needed by how much you do for them. INSTEAD, take risks on hurting their feelings, being direct and using strategies that change behavior.

Organizer role. Synchronize your watches. On your mark, get set—go! And so the rat race begins of organizing and coordinating *everything that happens in the family,* not just recreational activities. Organizers take charge because it's comfortable being in control and you know that you *will get it done.* Trust that promises are kept, appointments are punctual, and chores started are finished. Nothing is left to chance. No risks, no maybes, no relying on another family member who might goof things up. You're the CEO of family business. Orders come from the top and follow-through makes for a perfect household, but of course, only in theory. RESIST being the chief in command and loyally organizing everybody's schedule so it feels right. INSTEAD, trust other family members. Your spouse in particular. Ask that person to plan, take care of his or her personal business. Rotate with your spouse on who organizes the kids' schedule. And expect organization in the household to have its flaws.

How Can I Make Time for Myself and My Spouse?

First question is, "Do you want to?" It sounds like a rhetorical question because doesn't everybody? On the average: yes. But if you feel afflicted by the dirty roles you play in the family you might think differently. For now, though, let's take a positive approach and say making time for you and your spouse *is* desirable.

Squeezing in time for a taste of old fashioned lovin' really is not the solution. You and your spouse need private time together for many reasons besides sex. Otherwise, when would you discuss finances? Purchases? The kids? Or have time simply to hang around together? There is very little time to do that. Time is a scarce commodity and like brain cells it deteriorates without being replaced. That is why calculated efforts must be put into motion to reserve time for the marriage. Here are common interferences upon marital time and ways to get around them:

1.   *Bedtime is late.* Set early bedtime hours for your children instead of waiting until they are "ready" for sleep. Ages 1—3 years old put to bed around 7:00 p.m. Ages 4—6 put to bed around 7:30 to 8:00 p.m. Ages 7—10 put to bed 8:30 p.m. Ages 11—16 put to bed 9:00 p.m. to 10:00 p.m. Ages 17 to 18, bedtime is more flexible (up to 11:00 or 11:30). Naturally extenuating factors such illness, trips, sleepovers, and special house guests change these times.

2.   *Kids's weekly schedule is busy.* Carpools, homework, and volunteering in the kids' activities can get too crazy. Reserve one to two evenings a week and one evening on the weekend, devoted to

you and your spouse. That means rearranging the kids' schedule or other drivers.

3.   *Can't find a babysitter*. This is a very real problem. Baby–sitters are becoming an extinguished breed as more kids take jobs or plan early for college. Second, trust in babysitters is lower since there have been more charges of sexual misconduct across the nation. Third, with more working parents, babysitters are in constant demand, for longer hours. Fourth, today's moms and dads moved away from the homestead ruling out their own parents or relatives as backup babysitters. So, what is there to do?

a.   Find out the names and phone numbers of recent graduates of babysitting certification classes offered through American Red Cross.

b.   Find a retired couple or elderly single person willing to come to your home while you are out.

c.   Participate in community, church or synagogue babysitting co–ops. These are programs where you earn credit for babysitting that can be exchanged for time from another babysitter in the cooperative.

d.   Use babysitters more frequently. A young adult who can see earnings on a regular weekly or monthly basis may become more available.

e.   Check if the place you're going to has a babysitter. Many spas, clubs, even shopping malls now are financing hour by hour daycare facilities on the premises. Trust is hard with a stranger and your child may be hesitant. So start off easy and in short spans. Go to the spa for 1 hour instead of 2 hours. Wait to see what happens. Your children can adapt more easily to new situations than you can. Strange new toys, attention from adults, and other playmates are stimulating rewards. Then slowly increase the length of time they spend there.

f.   S.O.S. for help. S.O.S. or Sitters—On—Site is one among many national daycare and babysitting givers. S.O.S., started in East Lansing, Michigan, provides three different kinds of care: hourly (on–call), fulltime, and commercial. Commercial care is for families attending conventions or large gatherings from out of town. Hourly fees range from $6.50 to $8.00 per hour, with a minimum of 4 hours. Sitters go through a stiff screening process. Checked are letters of reference, criminal record, babysitting experience, maturity, and availability. Contact your local program for more details.

4.   *Kids are sick or injured.* Injury takes a toll of children worse than adults. Sickness is worse. Helplessly your child beckons your call with his coughs, sneezes and watery eyes. Pain they are in is pain you share. Babysitters are out of the question; and leaving the child alone feels cruel. How do you get around this problem? How about bringing in the adult fun. Night after night routines anchor you and your spouse into doing very little together. So, if you must stay home, crash the monotony with a little excitement. Get carryout food, VCR movies, play board games, or do something unusual.

5.   *Kids misbehave around other people.* Staying home happens for another reason. When you anticipate the kids' behavior being awful wherever you go, you don't want to go anywhere. You also resist hiring a babysitter or leaving the children with another person for fear of their misbehavior. How will they react? Will they scream, yell or run around like they do at home? Just thinking about these chances sours your

interest in a night on the town. But this fear goes away after risking a babysitter who agrees to your type of discipline. Talk to the sitter beforehand on strategies and potential problems. You'd be surprise how effective an outsider can be upon the kids. Give the sitter a try despite your past failures.

How Can I make Time for the Kids?

Stretching every second to last a lifetime is no easy task. Even balancing your own personal time with marital time is difficult. And where do the children fit in? How far can you stretch yourself before you burst? The answer: Very far, if it is done right. Kids get attention in all sorts of ways. Seizing these ways is the first step to making time for them. Nothing is hard about the following steps.

1.   *Look for what they do right.* It sounds funny. But do you realize how much precious time goes by without your child hearing a compliment? Look at what she is doing. Is the behavior harmless, appropriate, compliant, happy? If so, let your child know how good that behavior is. If it is anything close to being appropriate, compliment him with hugs, kisses or just verbal recognition.

Remember, it's easy to overlook good behavior for fear that by talking to your child he will start up his tantrum again. And that's a risk you'll have to take.

2.   *Talk to your children about feelings.* Feeling words such as bad, good, sad, mad, and happy all describe your child's world. Questions about feelings always draw kids and parents together. The one exception is with nonspeaking or preverbal children. "Feeling–talk" also is good around the meal table. After lunch or supper have a "family meeting." Here kids express opinions about themselves, each other, and about mom and dad, without recourse.

3.   *Give them opportunities for creativity and independence.* Closeness happens when children can run free (for a limited time) around new toys, people, and surroundings. Let kids explore events, shapes, sizes and foods on their own. Help them with creative tasks such as coloring, playing with Ninja Turtles, or even watching television (for a limited time) .

4. *Spend your domestic or chore time with kids.* Sounds easy enough to do but even easier to forget. When dusting furniture, making dinner, running to the hardware store or fixing the hydraulic, ask your child to keep you company. He might color, draw, help you out, or or do some independent silent activity, but he is still around you. That pleases his need for attention and assures some minimal time together.

5. *Establish basic routines.* Routines guarantee attention and bonding with little time cost. Select core times in the day or night when you can spend 10 to 30 minutes privately with one child. Like bedtime. Like bath time. Like when getting the kids dressed. Take precious time out of the task itself for affection, brief feeling words, and reviewing the day's fun events.

6. *Use humor.* Adult humor is one thing. Kid humor is another. It is different from "Baby talk." Baby talk is using a childish, cute voice when speaking to infants. Adults speak this way because they're not really sure how to speak to infants. And rarely is it humorous. Real humor is not stand up comedy. It begins with clever use of face, hands, and

voices. Like a magician, parents who make funny faces, tickle their children, and impersonate cartoon voices, get kids to laugh.

How To Let the Kids Become Independent

Trouble lurks in families where parents try too hard to make their kids happy. It's a strange dilemma. On the one hand you go out of your way to fix his bicycle, shuttle her around from dance class to soccer, and prepare a knock out meal for dinner. No matter how satisfied they are, needs keep on coming. Needs are insatiable.

Demands of marriage are tough enough but get severely complicated if all of your child's wishes take top priority as well. This is happiness *at your expense*. Happiness still can happen if you do less for your children. Backing off may raise a conflict or two, but children get the benefit of learning on their own––they become independent. Ways of developing independence for smaller kids are different from the ways for adolescents. First, take a look at what children need to develop independence:

1.   *Opportunities to learn any new toy without total guidance from parents.* Let the kids try them

out by themselves, without your direction all the time.

2. *Opportunities to make mistakes on any task, toy, or in daily situations.* Let kids fall, tumble, get dirty, or make errors even if you hate errors. It doesn't embarrass them like it might you. Mistakes are critical building blocks in learning new skills. The more mistakes made, the faster a child polishes a skill to mastery. It follows a corny but true formula, called the "3 E's":

EFFORT + ERROR = EXCELLENCE

3. *Opportunities to select rewards for being good or compliant.* Let kids choose what they want for rewards rather than what you think they want. Case in point regards the ever popular M & M's. One parent gave her child M & M's whenever he put his shoes away. But it only lasted a short time. He stopped putting away his shoes for no apparent reason. Except, of course, that after checking it out the mother discovered her son hated M & M's. Rule one, then, is let your child pick out his reward because only your child really knows what feels good.

4.   *Opportunities to select events, objects or activities among a host of options.* Just as picking rewards is healthy, so is giving your child choices about tasks, order of priorities, and with whom he would like to play. Choices make your child feel they own a piece of the rock; that they have some control over their actions.

Remember, *opportunities must be made available to children, prompts need to occur so children try new things. Children do not create opportunities on their own or know what to do with opportunities if just handed them.*

Independence for *adolescents* is a tricky thing. Part of maturity, of thinking for yourself, is being defiant, angry and resentful of your values. Your adolescent develops these characteristics in normal growth regardless of your prompts. Still, defiance and rugged "me first" ideas are not all bad as long as adolescents have the same opportunities as kids have, plus the following opportunities:

1.   *Opportunities to express feelings.* Always, always, always let your adolescent say his peace. You don't have to agree with it, nor argue against it. Saying what's on his mind is one thing, swearing

is another. Your child's opinions may contain abusive language which is inappropriate. Deal with that language after hearing what your son is saying. Whereas, not listening to your child instantly invites lying.

2.   *Opportunities for responsibility.* C a r privileges, babysitting or any small steps of adulthood earn an adolescent respect for being in control. Let your child assume new and simple adult responsibilities, cutting slack for mistakes.

3.   *Opportunity for risks.* Some adolescent responsibilities are risky. They involve staying out later hours, attending parties with "strange" friends, and wearing shirts, pants or outfits you wouldn't be caught dead in. Restricting these risks plants seeds of curiosity about these things behind your back, whereas approval of one or two of them shows compromise. It still may make your adolescent unhappy, but at least not defiant.

4.   *Opportunity for defending and accepting blame.* Conflict traps escalate when parents mistakenly think a child is undermining their authority. "Who does he think he is? She shouldn't say that to me!" But the irony is that your child probably would not be defensive if he thought you'd be lenient with his punishment.

Defensiveness hides the truth and protects an adolescent from looking bad. It delays punishment as well. The more accused the adolescent feels, expect a stronger dose of defensiveness. The less accused he is, defensiveness diminishes and confession begins. Let your adolescent get defensive until he sees it doesn't matter; what matters, or draws your attention, is disclosure of what really happened.

5.   *Opportunity to control situation.* Parents refuse this idea outright until they learn what it is. Your child needs experience with "control" as much as adults do. Find small ways around the house your child can be in charge of the situation. For instance, when returning home at night, let him push the garage door opener, or unlock the door with the key, or prepare his own sandwich for dinner. It's more than taking responsibilities. Little by little your child participates in the situation just like you do, imitating how you do it; until he can do it by himself. That kind of control teaches initiative and cooperation .

Working Parents

Many families today have two working parents. All types of jobs. Career jobs, temporary jobs, jobs in the house, and one spouse working for the other spouse. Nearly 40% of the American workforce are working parents earning a living to stay one step ahead of inflation. Do they do it? Sure they do. In fact, stories of rags to riches are countless. Take the Robinsons. At first Mr. Robinson, a General Motors employee making $25,000 for starters, was the only breadwinner. His wife stayed home while pregnant with son Bruce. After Bruce's birth, Mrs. Robinson landed a job at General Motors, at a different plant from her husband. Her salary was also about $25,000. Suddenly the Robinson's felt the financial windfall and relief from bills. No longer was the household budget operating on $25,000 a year—now it was $50,000 a year, which paid expenses and left plenty for fun.

The moral: *Two income family produces more opportunity for adult and family growth.* Spouses who pool their salaries step into that affordable range of luxury, not millions, but more money and the incentive to keep that money flowing remains strong. That is why it is so hard to give up one job to raise a child. And what if the veteran working parent, main bread winner, is the wife? Why should *she* sacrifice her vested job just for the sake of tradition of mom's raising the kids? The answer is clear: She shouldn't. But for moms and dads there are loads of questions facing this problem. Let's consider the more popular ones.

How Can I Not Feel Guilty?

Guilt and shame are normal to feel. Trying to get away from all remorse is like starving. It can't be done unless you plan on hurting your body. That's why anorexia fails—it hurts the body. Saying, "I won't feel guilty for working and leaving my children at a daycare" is the same thing. You feel more hurt from pretending there is no guilt than by recognizing it and dealing with it. Determine your guilt quotient. Do you feel any of these are true?

1. I am a bad parent for deserting my child during his early years.
2. I am a bad parent for ruining the bond between parent and child.
3. I am a bad parent for being selfish and thinking only of my job.

Answers of "true" mean you dislike your decision for work and believe your place really is at home. That your child really cannot survive without you being there. That is, physical and emotional growth feeds off of your breathing words and direction. But guess what. That's not entirely true. The good and bad about staying home is this: *the more you stay home, the less you grow as an adult. Your life does not stand still while children develop. Development for both parent and child is a simultaneous process.*

In chapter 8 on daycare, the pros and cons of staying home versus daycare are clearer. For now, consider that guilt is like a warning signal triggered inside your mind whenever you feel *bad things* will happen to your child by leaving her for work. Worries that your child will:

1.　Grow up to hate parents.
2.　Grow up to hate adults.
3.　Grow up to be a delinquent or criminal.
4.　Grow up to disobey rules.
5.　Grow up to hate girls or boys.
6.　Grow up to be too independent and become a hermit.

7.   Grow up to be too assertive, too selfish and not caring.

8.   Grow up to disobey rules.

You've plotted it out. Like Nostradamus, you can predict the future hazards experienced by your child if you abandon him during child rearing years. And all of this frantic worry is based on one thing: *Fear*. Fear that *you failed as a parent and will never be able to repair the damage*. This is scary, no doubt. Nobody wants a problem child, frequent calls from the principal, or later trouble with the juvenile court system. That is not what having children was for. It was for building a loving family, not for earning your apprenticeship in social work and law. Fear stigmatizes you into thinking you'll be the laughing stock of the neighborhood and a lousy parent.

But don't panic. There's a twist to this problem. Fear that all will go haywire is inflating a normal reaction to parental pressure. All parents feel this pressure. The pressure is that, staying home or working, mistakes in parenting must be avoided at all costs. But why? Why can't you make mistakes? Why can't things go wrong—not just once, twice, or three times. But many times? It's part of experimenting, learning, and developing confidence in parenthood. And one type of development needed for parenthood is learning to risk new things that seem wrong or selfish.

Fear disappears when parents risk doing things that seem wrong or frightening but once they are done turn out just fine. And working is one of those risks. Taking a job or returning to work weeks after birth is a risk that builds your own strength and teaches children adjustment in wonderful ways. All the horrible things you worry will happen never really happen and the time spent with your children before work, after work or on weekends tends to be more productive and genuine than if either spouse stayed around the kids for 24 hours.

How Can I Balance Priorities?

When does your day start? At 5:00 am, 6:00 am, or later? What do you do at this hour? For working parents the weekday starts with a kick–in–the–pants, coffee awakening burst of energy to get ready for the job. Even sluggish, sleepy eyed parents finally get around to lifting an eyelid by the 7:00 a.m. hour if their jobs begin by 8:00 a.m. Morning time also is a busy time. Get the kids up, dressed, breakfast in their stomachs, and out to the bus stop or in the car shuttle to daycare. It all moves on a rapid time schedule.

And by the time you or your spouse arrive at work, sit at your desk or station and breathe a sigh of relief, it hits: Did I say hello to my child this morning? Did I kiss him? Did I even look at her this morning? Where was I? And what did they do? *Did I miss them completely?* Speed of morning routines swipes valuable moments of parent–child interaction and the next family time must wait until early evening. This is a bummer. It gets aggravating waiting 8 hours just to kiss your child again or ask him how his swimming classes were two days ago. That's why priorities must be shuffled about in proper order. In a balanced order.

Balancing priorities is part time management and part child management. Time managing is the easier part, naturally, because it's something you can do without the kids' help. Managing your child is tougher because they have to cooperate. Take the first one—time. Arrange your priorities with the kids so that in the morning or evening or on weekends the most important things for them are done before playtime. Consider this order of priorities:

Health
Clothing
School
Family
Social

Health. These priorities are medical, dental, or mental health related concerns or appointments. They rank first because without functional health your child's ability to handle anything else is jeopardized.

Clothing. Fitting your child with right size clothing and new shoes determines her comfort during the day. Tightly fit clothing pulls, tears and disturbs concentration no matter where your child is that day.

School. Once physical needs are in order, next highest ranking priority is education. All aspects of education pertain here, from teachers' conferences to school supplies, to completing homework, to meetings with principals. Conferences on disciplinary actions or curriculum planning (some states call these *IEPCs*) must be attended to show support for your child and respect for school efforts.

Family. When priorities ahead of this are met, family fun begins. This is anything and everything between mom, dad, and kids. Visits to parks, museums, auto shows, even camping or going on vacations make up fun. Visits to relatives, to grandma and grandpa, to uncles, aunts, and cousins follow right along. Some activities have precise dates in the calendar and others spontaneously arise out of the spur of the moment. But it's the second type that parents usually forget to do.

Spontaneous fun. After work or on weekends are good times for this. You've always wanted to do this and many parents already do it. It's a matter of remembering, risk–taking and just trying to loosen up. Saying, "c'mon, guys, let's all get in the car and take a drive." Or another spontaneous activity involving restaurants or in–house games that breaks up the day or night routine. Just "doing things" can also be simple. You can lay down next to your daughter while she watches television. You can join in their imaginary worlds of play with Ninja Mutant Turtles, Barbie, Muppet Babies, or G.I. Joe. You can sing songs with them or play an instrument while they play. But whatever spontaneously you decide to do—*do something that is quick, fun, and is rewarding to your child.*

Emphasis is upon *rewarding to your child.* How easy is it to recruit your son or daughter in projects you and only you benefit from? They stand there holding the sewing thread or the nails and lumber while you do the labor. And for what? Because that way you'll feel better they are around you? Does that satisfy the need for "doing something with them?" I hope not. That's the wrong way to do it. Spontaneous fun that only is fun for mom or dad but not for kids is not spontaneous fun. It's boring and builds resentment. Stick as much as possible with what they like— you'll be surprised how quickly you'll like it too.

Social. Last priority is social and peer activities. Part of sharing time with your children is when they play with other children. Volunteer in the brownie, girl scouts, cub scouts, boy scouts meetings. Volunteer to bring cookies or help on field trips (job permitting) and especially if any trip or group outing is on weekends.

How Can I Get My Own Free Time?

Well, one thing is for certain. You can't buy time for yourself. There's already little to go around and it gets even slimmer. Even shuffling kids here and there according to priorities still may squeeze your personal time so thin that it doesn't exist. And no time for yourself is like no sleep. One sleepless night is minor. Two sleepless nights is irritating. By the third night you're a sure cast member of the *Night of the Living Dead*. You feel angry, irate, stalking any child prey who dares to cross you. Deprived and resentful, you scowl at every chore, every responsibility to your family and start daydreaming about cruises to the Caribbean. Anything—even wishful thinking, just to escape the imprisonment of helping others.

A five day or more work week takes a toll on parents. It's emotionally draining and physically tiresome. And child demands deplete what little strength you have left. One way of raising the spirit in you is knowing you arranged time for yourself, somewhere in the busy schedule, no matter what the selfish activity is. Riding your bicycle, reading a book, working on the computer, sewing, attending coupon—club meetings or choirs. Any of these will do. But there must be *something to do for yourself.* Here are the best ways to set aside personal time:

1.   Arrange with your spouse one or two nights a week for you to attend activities of your choice.

2.   Arrange with your spouse one to two hours a night, either before or after kids go to bed, for personal activities.

3.   Establish an activity that can be worked on and interrupted every day or frequently during the week. Let it have a definite starting and end point.

4.   Establish a balance with spouse on what you will do for him or her in return for the time you have for yourself.

How Can I Make My Spouse Help Out?

Naturally there is one slight difficulty with any of these ideas. What if your spouse doesn't help out? What if he or she resists your compromises and denies your need for private time? Making you be fulltime parent on top of your workload is more than slavery. It's pushing the panic button. You'll hear ringing in your ears and thoughts repeated over and over that say, "that's not fair," "that's not fair," "that's not fair." And you're right. It's not. But what can you do about it?

First, let's talk about what you *shouldn't do*. Even the best intentioned parents slip into these traps under duress. Desperation for private personal time at any expense can start bad habits or risks beyond control that feel right for the moment but leave a trail of trouble for yourself, your spouse and the kids. Ask yourself if you've done any of these things to get away:

DON'T DO THIS:

1. Hide in your bedroom or anywhere in the house for 2 or more hours. Refuse to let any soul in.
2. Drink 2 or more beers or mixed drinks to relax you around the kids and spouse.
3. Smoke pot to relax you around the kids and spouse.
4. Eat your way through the kitchen to relax around the kids and spouse.
5. Need or demand sex to feel relaxed.
6. Yell and act so angry that everybody stays clear of your path.
7. Engross yourself in television, a book or music and ignore others around you.
8. Cry your heart out or look depressed so everybody gives you sympathy and then leaves you alone.

Slipping into these avoidance and escape patterns can get out of hand in no time. Before you realize it, you're doing all this weird, bizarre behavior just for peace and quiet and soon it backfires on you. Instead of peace and quiet, you're developing horrible habits which hurt you and distance you from the family.

Self–hurt also happens when you try "ingenious" ways of manipulating your spouse into sparing you personal time. You forfeit logical discussion and problem–solving for a quick and dry, beat around the bush solution. It saves time, saves conflict, and might, just might, even accelerate what you want without all the nasty steps in between. What do these beat around the bush solutions include? Ask yourself if you do these things:

DON'T DO THESE THINGS EITHER:

1.   Have sex when your spouse wants it or the way that person wants it to get your way.

2.   Go overboard to please your spouse, from extra, extra special treats or meals or money everyday, every night—to saying "yes, of course I will," when you want to say "no, no way."

3.   Go along with your spouse on decisions, purchases or even child discipline tactics against your better judgment.

4.   Lie, cheat or do things behind your spouse's back but maintain an innocent face.

These deceptive tactics are more than harmful to the marriage and family. They make you hate yourself and your situation. Fear of charging into the lion's den with your personal needs is not your spouse's fault—*it's your fault. It's your fault for being afraid to speak up for yourself and believe in your needs.* You can take the bull by the horn and crank out solutions without hurting yourself if you want to and if your personal time means that much to you. Here's what to do if your spouse says "no" to your needs:

DO THIS INSTEAD:

1.   *Describe* exactly what you want and when you want it.

Express how you feel about what you want.

Specify what your spouse needs to do to help you get what you want.

Specify what your spouse can get from you   for doing this favor.

It goes like this:

Describe: I'd like 2 hours alone tonight for cutting coupons.

Express: The kids interrupt me and I lose my concentration. So, I want to do it alone.

Specify: How about it if you watch them from 6:00 to 8:00 tonight.

Specify: If you do, then we can watch TV together afterwards. But if you don't, I'll probably be unpleasant to be around all night. And, I don't think I'll be so willing to sit for you when you want time away.

2.   Okay. But what if your spouse tricks you. He or she says, "so, big deal. See if I care how mad you get. I won't do it." Then what do you do? Here's an option:

Say: That's not the point. The point is that I want you to watch the kids for 2 hours while I cut coupons. Then we can do something together. Watch TV or whatever.

(DANGER ZONE: make sure the "or whatever" is something you agree to, not what you consent to just to get your way or manipulate your spouse.)

3. That's better. But it still doesn't take the prize. Your spouse gets angry, maybe teases you, maybe accuses you, maybe says or does things that turns it around and makes you look like a lazy, irresponsible person. What if your spouse says or does the following things?

> a. "God, you look funny when you get serious." (makes fun of you)
>
> b. "Who do you think you are demanding these things?" (accuses you)
>
> c . "Don't you ask me again or I'll..." (threatens you)
>
> d. "Yea, and what about tomorrow, or will you change your mind tonight, and for how long?" (argues with you)
>
> e. Yells at you.
>
> f. Walks away from you.

Reactions like these are called "roadblocks" They roadblock you from getting your point across. They also interrupt your train of thought and dismantle your needs until you surrender to defeat.

That is, *if* you surrender to defeat. Here's what to do instead.

4.   *Repeat*:   That's not the point, the point is that I want you to babysit while I cut coupons. Because you won't help me out here, I will not help you out the next time you need me to babysit.

And you must follow through on your threat. Do not forfeit it unless your spouse does something you asked him or her to do with the kids in the immediate future, like that evening or next morning.

It's true. You may feel you lost the battle. "But my spouse still got away with it. I lose, he or she wins!" *Wrong. Nobody wins or loses. It's not a contest. It's a learning situation.* Your spouse may refuse doing what you ask, so your personal time goes out the window. But your spouse also learns an important lesson about you. That you will not stand for "no I won't" without putting up a fuss. Your spouse will experience this outcome when he or she really needs you and you say, "hey, sorry."

Is that spite? I thought "two wrongs don't make a right?" Is that being mean and only frustrating the marriage more? It feels like it, doesn't it? It feels like if you get back at your spouse later, that only gives that person more reason to deny your favors again and again. Right? *No, not right.* That's not how human behavior works. It works like this:

When people want something, they'll make sacrifices or change behavior to get it, even if that change is something they resisted in the past. But if they see they can get what they want without sacrifices and behavior change, then sacrifices and changes never happen.

The approach is straight forward. If you lay out in no uncertain terms the positive and negative outcomes for your spouse letting you have private time, you'll probably get your private time. If your spouse balks or refuses you, follow through on negative outcomes no matter what you think he or she will do "to retaliate." They only retaliate or get angry because they are not accustomed to you being direct, consistent, and wise to their tricks.

Single Parents

Single parents represent the fastest growing segment of parenting population in the 1990's. It's not unusual to see a single mother or father raising children while juggling the fast lane demands of employment. Singlehood happens for many reasons. From a divorce, from spouse death, from foster adoptions (without marriage), or from custody placements. Grandparents fall into this category as well, if they raise a child left from deaths of the mother and father. Or the court may appoint custody of children to grandparents given the natural mother or father's mental illness, substance abuse, or physical disability. It takes many shapes and forms, but the rapid growth of one parent doing the duty of two parents is a serious matter. And the questions faced by this challenge are many. Like, for instance:

How Do I Play Both Mom and Dad?

You don't. Don't even try dual roles because it will confuse the kids even more. Ask yourself, "what do kids need exposure to for a well- rounded experience?" Kids need exposure to fun, curious, creative and stimulating activities as much as to rigid, structured and even boring activities. Activities should be physical, recreational, as well as problem solving, thinking, and task oriented. Exposure to rough, rugged masculine toys and sports is good for both girls and boys. So is delicate, soft, doll playing and quiet time spent coloring, painting, or in make believe.

In other words, think of yourself as a teacher. School teachers are both men and women. Men teachers offer students as much unisexual experience as do women teachers. That's your role. Your daughter or son will not *miss* the opposite sex spouse in terms of learning to do what that gender typically does if you make sure experiences are diverse. Think like a teacher who makes sure children do a little of everything.

Your children also have many opportunities to see men and women adults in school, in groups and organizations, in church and synagogue, and with their grandparents. They will not lack contact with adult men and women or lose out on precious insider knowledge about their gender. Your mission is allowing for these opportunities to happen with great frequency.

How Do I Introduce My "Date" to the Kids?

Very carefully. Single parents, particularly working parents who have little free time, bargain with babysitters for brief interludes when they can be alone and keep their lives moving. Career growth is one thing. Life growth is another. Time flies when hour after hour is devoted to waiting on children and trying to anticipate the next crisis. It loads you down emotionally and interferes with re–building a social life. That's why when you finally meet somebody new, somebody who fills that void of loneliness, time becomes even more scarce. You suddenly cannot separate kids from social life. There's just not enough time in the day or week to do that.

So, what happens? The final countdown. Godzilla meets the Thing. There's no escaping it. Time is now to introduce your special friend to the kids. And be ready for any number of reactions. Your kids might do these things:

1. Withdrawal, act very quiet around person.
2. Act aggressively, angry outbursts around person.
3. Try attention-seeking actions around person.
4. (adolescent) Ask obnoxious questions of person.
5. (adolescent) Embarrass you with rude or insulting statements.

That sweet, respectful, kind, loving and charming child you raised suddenly transforms into any number of extremes. Hello Mr. Hyde and Dr. Jekyll. And the reasons are simple. Your children do not know how to react to a boyfriend or girlfriend. Even adolescent children are suspicious, curious, and afraid. Will this person steal away their bread and butter? Will this person pretend they are something they are not; like being a mother or father? Younger children may warm up to your date faster out of naivete and through your encouragement. Adolescent children may remain distant, appear offensive, and resist warm overtures from your special friend.

So, how do you handle this? End the relationship? Heavens, no. Don't do that. And don't do these things either.

DON'T:

1.   Decide the kids hate your friend so the relationship will never work; if you do that, you quickly build resentment toward your children for sabotaging your friendships and lovers.

2.   Pacify your resistant children with gifts, money or promises as long as they behave nicely to your friend; doing this places a price tag on the

relationship. If that relationship continues and turns into marriage potential, your kids will always expect something for being civil in his or her company.

3.   Force friendships upon the children by insisting they behave or lose privileges; very dangerous. Now your kids will pair this new friend with punishment and always be angry around him.

4.   Blame your kids behavior on your friend; this only disguises your fears of failure, vulnerability, and unwillingness to deal with the children. It also threatens loss of a potentially good relationship.

5.   Blame your kids behavior on yourself; why torture yourself? Resistance, anger, or attention seeking are normal reactions and should be expected instead of personalizing this problem as your own failure.

So, what's the right way? There are many tricks of the trade in introducing Mr. Right or Mrs. Right to the family. Here are the best ways:

1.   *Be honest.* Tell your children (ages 2—8) this is a new friend and that you (mommy, daddy) say its "okay" to talk to this person (his or her name).

2.   *Arrange the first meeting to involve time spent with the children and yourself in a situation familiar and rewarding to the children.* Almost so that the children do not notice the person is even there. Watch television, a video movie, play Nintendo, or eat meals in the house. Activities the children usually do and can feel comfortable in.

3.   Following #2 above, *have your friend play with the kids in their activities instead of creating new topics for discussion.* Questions like, "So, Billy, I hear you play baseball. Do you like baseball?" are perplexing. Billy thinks, "Gee, mom never asks me this, why is this guy asking me?" Your friend, in other words, should duplicate the *voice, style or behavior of you as you interact with the kids.* The closer he or she looks, sounds or behaves like the role model, the faster the person blends in.

4.   *NEVER, NEVER, NEVER have the person on the first, second or even first month of meetings do your job as disciplinarian.* Don't risk it. That

means always being there with your friend and the kids. Having him or her babysit for the kids is also out of the question. The main reason is this: Strangers already frighten children. If you allow this stranger to discipline them, your kids will not know if they should listen to him or her. Listening to what the persons says might go against what you taught them around strangers. "If a stranger asks you into his car, don't listen to him; it will make me angry if you go with that stranger." So, they may not listen to your special friend because it might make you angry.

5.   *Slowly introduce your friend's children to your children.* Too much too soon is the problem. All together in the same room for the first time puts pressure on everybody. Naturally you will want to be sweet to your friend's kids. But your kids might be angry at that, might act out against your friend or his kids, or remain very quiet. Instead, first establish rapport between your friend and your kids, before introducing other actors onto the stage.

Will My Kids Be More Masculine or Feminine?

"I don't want a sissy!" "Yea, and I don't want a tomboy!" Cries of fear shriek out of parents mouths at the mere thought of raising children who take on "too many qualities" of the opposite sex. Fears are that boys raised by mothers may only play with dolls or stay in the kitchen. Fears are that girls raised by fathers will be couch potatoes holding a beer in one hand, and a pretzel in the other, watching Monday night Football on the tube. Are these stereotypes true?

No, not really. What is true is that children take after their parents and behave in ways guided by the parents. So, if you only expose your child to heavy-duty, man-handling, greasy chores, that is exactly what your child considers life is all about; heavy-duty, man-handling, greasy chores. Boy or girl—it doesn't matter. Earlier the advice was *diversity*. The same advice holds true here, as well. Exposure to many different activities, traditionally masculine or feminine, is best for children so they can balance their skills and adjust to all situations.

What doubly sours the notes on this approach are friends, family or even that special new friend who disagrees with diversity. Statements like "He should be playing football, not playing with Ninja Turtles." Or, "Don't you realize that if she swings the bat like that she'll never learn to cook?" Advice people give is spiked with stereotypes and old fashioned beliefs that boys and girls have definite roles in society and mixing them up will lead to mixed up kids. But not true. Versatility will not lead to insanity. As a dear friend who lived in Manhattan once told me, anything goes as far as the likes of men and women; *time was you could tell the difference between them. Now, one looks like the other in appearance, behavior, and life goals.*

So, no matter what the peanut gallery says, always remember that tomorrow's world is more unisexual and nonsexist than ever existed in the past. The kids made to follow boy/girl stereotypes will be the ones who struggle. The diverse kids will be the normal ones.

Divorced Parents

Nobody likes a divorce. And nobody wins in divorce. Whether divorce came after a period of separation or was abrupt, it dismantles the family system. Wife, husband and children suffer. The toughest part of divorce is *who gets the kids?* Custody decisions become fierce if parents squabble over these rights and start accusing the other of abusive, neglectful or inadequate parenting. It becomes worse if custody is the by–product of ongoing conflict, started way before separation or divorce began. And what perplexes children beyond belief is not knowing who is right, who to believe, or why some other strangers (lawyers, case worker, friend of the court, etc.) are deciding these things for them.

Decisions in the form of *legal custody* (legal, financial decisions affecting children) or *physical custody* (physical residence of children) make up major battles that usually boil over in the way kids are treated in the aftermath. When the ink dries and the divorce decree speaks the law, does the bickering just fade away? Do things just get back to normal? No, because there is no more normal—at least the ways things used to be normal. Now the world for the family and children is different. They may live with one parent but visit another parent. And what about when they come back from that visit. That's the first of two problems facing divorced parents:

How Do I Cool My Child Down After A Visitation?

Horror story upon horror story has been heard about the late night monster who returns home violently aggressive and preys upon its innocent victims. These stories are talking about children returning from weekend visits with another parent. Upon return the child's behavior is wild, noncompliant, tantruming, and verbally insulting. That it takes 3 to 5 days minimum to house break this behavior and restore the child's manner. Home returns are usually messy for many reasons:

1.   Parenting practices between homes are inconsistent.

2.   Parenting practices of visited spouse are heavily punitive.

3.   Parenting practices of visited spouse are lenient or nonexistent.

4.   Parenting practices are done by someone besides the visited spouse.

5.   Parenting practices of visited spouse deviate from the regular meal, sleeping or habitual

schedules of the children. So when they go there, adjustment is like going to another planet.

6.   Parenting practices of visited spouse deviate morally, religiously or children are exposed to bizarre or inappropriate situations (e.g., pornography, substance abuse, theft, gambling, etc.).

Affected by these factors, children are not sure how to behave. For the two or three days exposed to a vastly different lifestyle they adjusted to new things the best they could. Now they are expected to shift gears right away in the home court. But children, young and adolescent, cannot do this. It's not like turning the light switch on and off. Adults can do this. An adult can walk into a room full of people and paste a smile on his face, but walk out of the room and drop the fake smile. Children simply lack that skill. They put the smile on their faces and keep it there until forced to take it off. It doesn't come off automatically. It comes off slowly.

This is because *when children must adjust quickly to new things, they can do it. And it remains the way they do things until they slow their pace down, become re-familiar with house* cues, and get back into the habit of doing things the way they used to (before visitation).

A mistake made is becoming angry. You lose your temper when your sweet, charming child runs around the house in a tirade, sounding like a siren on a fire truck. He runs upstairs and downstairs and is one step ahead of your escalating loud voice. But this anger only worsens his behavior. It feeds into the attention–seeking fire that was started and kept going while at the other spouse's house. You're only making it worse.

You can shorten the re–adjustment step after a visit by following these steps:

DO THIS:

1.   Immediately upon returning home (day or night), have your child go upstairs, take a bath (or you administer it), and change clothes.

2.   Second, plan a slow, quiet rewarding activity your child can do alone. If you must be around your child, plant him or her nearby while you remain busy.

3.   One to two hours later, have your child eat something while talking to you about the visit, or

anything he wants to talk to you about. If it is nighttime, have a brief conversation while your child lays in bed. Then let your child go to sleep.

4.   (Morning or afternoon) After the talk, ask your child the things he needs to do that week: for school, chores around the house, places they're going to, and things they want to do.

5.   Wait an hour, still having your child stay around the house in a slow, quiet activity. Then ask your child to do some task, chore or thing you want him to do, letting him know the good things he can get for doing it.

Let the day move at a slow, easy pace, without excitement or busy schedules. When behavior flares up, follow strategies talked about in earlier chapters on tantrums and not following instructions. As your child gets re-familiar with the house, is doing things you ask him to do, the strange new behaviors learned on the weekend fade into oblivion.

How Do I Talk To My "Ex" About Child Problems?

Very delicately. The toughie here is imposing your own preferences on your ex– spouse, who is unwilling to hear or accept anything you say. Of course, not all the time. Many marital splits are friendly. Couples divorce because they drifted apart or due to extenuating circumstances no longer could live together. But they maintain good communication. They can speak, listen, and compromise without fear of retaliation or loss of control. Vulnerability is not the focus of their exchanges.

But this is the rare case. Most divorced couples are protective of looking stupid, and of surrendering too much, too quick or being victimized again and again and again. This is particularly visible where one spouse used or currently uses drugs, is alcoholic, or is physically abusive. Anger sprays its deadly darts across the phone lines in every exchange, since face– to– face contact is already minimal. Fear is intense. The abused spouse still vividly remembers the fear, pain, and trauma suffered and absolutely distrusts the ex–spouse on everything he or she says or does. "No way, no how." Communication is rare and primarily through outsider channels like Friend of the Court or the attorneys.

But eventually it has to happen. If the ex–spouse has any visitation (with or without supervision) and if that visitation is on his or her own home turf, child problems may surface that must be talked about. That is why a strategy is in order. Here is how to notify your ex-spouse of the need to discuss a child's behavior problem. Also, note the steps for what to do once the discussion gets underway.

IF COMMUNICATION WITH EX–SPOUSE IS FRIENDLY

1. Call your ex–spouse on the phone and arrange a mutual day, time and location (your home or his) to discuss problem.

2. Outline a list of problems, things you request your ex-spouse to do, and what you can do as solutions.

3. Agree upon another day, time and location in 2 to 3 months to follow up on your mutual efforts and observations of your child's behavior.

4. Agree also, under an emergency or if there are behavior questions, to call one another for a

brief discussion about that emergency or behavior question.

IF COMMUNICATION WITH EX-SPOUSE IS HOSTILE

1.   Contact Friend of the Court or other established mediator. Explain the need for a meeting jointly held between you and your ex-spouse to discuss your child's behavior problems and parenting needs. Offer dates and times that you are available for the meeting. Follow up that phone call with a brief letter thanking Friend of Court for setting up the meeting and that you look forward to working things out with your ex-spouse.

But what if Friend of the Court refuses to be bothered, or hold the meeting? Then what?

Alternative 1: Contact your lawyer who should mediate a meeting between you and your ex-spouse. Let your attorney make the arrangements to be held at his office.

Alternative 2: Contact your pastor, minister, rabbi, or clergy and see if he or she might mediate. Again, follow the same steps in setting up an appointment and sending a letter confirming the meeting.

2.   Come prepared at the meeting with an outline of the problem and things you want you and your ex–spouse to change as solutions. Also, state ground rules at the beginning of the meeting. These ground rules are that:

  a.   Let's stick only with the topic of our child.

  b.   Let's not blame, accuse or throw verbal punches at the other person.

  c.   Let's move toward solutions, not anger.

  d.   Let's let the mediator do his or her job of conducting the meeting.

3.   If verbal assaults start anyway, immediately inform the mediator that this breaks the ground rules. Explain that you will be happy to continue once the assaults stop and we get back to the topic.

4.   When solutions are found, you and your ex–spouse agree to try new things, and ask to make another appointment *before you leave the*

mediator's office. Schedule an appointment 2—3 months in the future for review of the solutions.

5.   After the meeting is over and you're back home, send a brief letter to the mediator and your ex–spouse summarizing the solutions, or what both you and your ex–spouse plan on doing differently. Also remind them of the next meeting date. The last paragraph of the letter should say the following:

"This is my understanding of what took place during our meeting on (month/day/year). Should you disagree with any of the points listed here, please let me know in writing what they are. If I do not hear from you, I will assume these points are correct. "

God, what a pain! All that writing, formal talking like its a political campaign. Just to work out a behavior problem? There must be another way. *No, there's not.* Oh, sure. You can save yourself time, energy and money by calling your ex–spouse directly and pretending he or she will be decent on the phone with you. You can tolerate the abuse, the accusations, the name calling and possibly get a word in edgewise, only to hate this person all over again after you slam the receiver down on the phone. *But is it worth it?* No, it's not. It's never worth dumping yourself into a pile of garbage thinking that this time, maybe this time, you'll come out smelling like a rose. Changes do occur, and maybe one day communication between you and your ex-spouse may be friendly. But right now it isn't. And don't pretend it is. It's not an easy way out.

Step–Parenting

You probably thought after the divorce things would quiet down a bit. No more hassles. No more apologizing for mistakes. No more feeling guilty or always trying to organize the world. Finally, peace and quiet. Just what the doctor ordered.

But then the craziest thing happens. You meet someone. You see this person again, again, and again, opening up yourself slowly and cautiously. You will not make the same mistake twice. The closer it gets, the more *intimate* it becomes: secrets are shared, personal habits exposed, and months away plans of marriage are set.

Your children now know this person. He or she visits you regularly, takes time with the children and, using suggestions offered earlier, the two of you pair together for rewarding family activities. But this person is still a stranger in your home, an intruder the children may distrust. Knowing this, your efforts double with vigor. Outings with you, your friend, and the kids pick up pace, and your friend now attends immediate and extended family functions, holiday meals, and the kids' school events.

You even go so far as letting the kids rely on your friend. "Call him if you have an emergency at school or for a ride." Your friend acquires a parenting status only you had before. And as your kids reach out to this new parent, cautiously accepting his help, bonding builds into a solid trust. The kids ask him for advice, rush to his side for affection, enroll him in playtime, and wait for his permission on requests. At night, once he leaves the house, your kids even ask if he is returning. They start asking *questions. Many questions.* Like, "where does he work," "where does he live?," "does he have kids, too?" and "was he also married?"

Question after question, your kids sense this person slowly weaving into the family fabric. They ask whether he has dogs, cats, or does he like dogs and cats. Does he always wear his hair that way or why you like him. Questions ramble on so quickly, in all directions, that you assume the kids like your friend. *They must like him, otherwise why ask all these questions?* And so you let the cat out of the bag and say, "hey guess what guys, he asked me to marry him."

You're hit with silence. The kids say nothing. The room is quiet. Questions come to a shrieking halt. You feel *something is wrong*. In a way you're right. The excitement surrounding this stranger who turns personal friend, for the children, is like bringing home a new toy or pet. Play with it, learn about it, even make it a best friend, *but then go on to something new*. Marriage means *he* stays around a long time. This permanency hits children even stronger when special friends move in and live with your family.

Into the marriage or months after living together, those same energetic, affectionate, full-of- questions kids are doing a Dr. Jekyll and Mr. Hyde routine. But there are important reasons why this happens.

Problems To Watch Out For

Stepfamilies put a new strain on your family. Besides one new face in the morning, kids must adjust to how this person differs from yourself or from your ex-spouse. Adjustment is never easy. And different ages of children determine types of problems you may encounter. Let's consider what all the children, regardless of age, will experience and strategies you can take to eliminate the problem.

Common Problems

Problem 1.   Pressure on your child to forget your ex–spouse and accept the new person.

Solution: Emphasize the value of loving their mother or father and being obedient to this person when with them. Even participate in meetings with your ex–spouse, with your kids present, verbalizing how important this love is. Let your child also know the relationship with your new spouse should be like having a *best friend*.

Problem 2. Pressure on your child for feeling responsible for the divorce, or absence of ex–

spouse. Guilt, lack of love or fear may make him believe he disrupted the family.

Solution: Ask your child to talk about her feelings. Be specific that mommy and daddy split up because of their own reasons. In cases of death, be specific that dying is a natural part of life and that the deceased spouse is not angry at that child or anybody else. Tragic accidents of course make this solution more difficult. But children must verbally say aloud that they are not the blame for bad things happening.

Problem 3.   Pressure on your child living under your roof with this stranger and still being loyal to the ex– spouse during visitation. Particularly when the stepfamily is new and pieces are just forming together, your ex–spouse's curiosity or jealousy may mean he or she pumps the kids for every ounce of information about the stepfamily. Your children accidentally become messengers, spies, and secret agents.

Solution: Confront your ex-spouse at once. Let him or her know that the kids are not voyeurs; they cannot be set up to peep into the new marriage, or stepfamily only to report the findings at a later time. Remind your ex– spouse to ask you, not the kids, about this information. When it persists despite your friendly warning, contact may be necessary through Friend of the Court or your attorney. As for the kids, teach them to refuse being a spy by rehearsing with them certain words or phrases in response to pleas by your ex–spouse.

Problem 4. Pressure on your children to meet, accept or at least be cordial to new people who know your friend. Faces such as your friend's children, parents, (new grandparents), relatives, and associates.

Solution: Let these experiences be slow, gradual and rewarding. Like introducing your friend, contacts should be short, at first fewer, and enjoyable. It also is helpful explaining to your children that these new people are strangers but *they can talk to them* . If your kids pull away from hugs, kisses or touching by your new spouse's friends and relatives, let it happen. Do not apologize for them or become angry over it. This is a very delicate process which cannot be rushed. If you rush it, kids can resent your new spouse and be horribly defiant.

Problem 5. Pressure on your children to love, cherish and obey your new friend (spouse) as much as you do. But children do not take the same marriage vows. In fact, shortly before your wedding or even shortly thereafter, your kids will fantasize about you and your ex– spouse remarrying.

Solution: Let the kids know they never have to forget or dislike your ex–spouse. Let them know it is okay to just be friends with your new spouse. Focus is upon *trying out the relationship just like you want your children to try many new things.*

Problem 6. Pressure on your children to love both sets of parents equally. When visitation with ex–spouse or his or her family is active, children feel confused over who to listen to about discipline. Your ex–spouse says one thing, but it contradicts what your new husband or wife says. *Who should the children obey?*

Solution: The best solution lies with letting the children ask questions and point out when there are clear disagreements.

Problem 7.   Pressure on your children to meet the *new* expectations of their new parent. By now the kids developed some sense of what you expect from them, and even how they must behave around your ex–spouse. But what if expectations for good behavior are radically different between you and your new spouse?

Solution: Find out what your new spouse thinks of children, of discipline and agree on strategies to use.

Problem 8.   Pressure on your children to always be up, energetic and never shy. This is unfortunate because it never happens. Kids react to stepfamilies by withdrawing, by hiding in their rooms, or by sudden silence. Personality shifts can be subtle or quite dramatic.

Solution: For withdrawn behavior, set up situations between your child and new spouse where they can do mutually rewarding activities.

Be sure your child is talking or participating in the situation. Be sure your new spouse is listening or playing along in the situation. Second, teach your child to ask your new spouse general questions, opinions, or seek his or her input on decisions.

Problem 9. Pressure on your children to be obedient to whatever your new spouse says. But just the opposite happens. Anger, defiance, and serious behavioral problems can arise in the first months to the first two years in stepfamilies. Talking back is the most shocking behavior to handle because your new spouse *is not used to it and wants desperately to be accepted by your kids* He or she in turn may react the wrong way: by yelling, screaming, arguing, or threatening loss of privileges. What makes it all a nightmare is that these punishers never were necessary until the stepfamily started.

Solution: First, sort out all the wrong assumptions your new spouse is making about the kids. Teach him or her to look at the *behavior, not the person, and not to take it all personally.* Second, teach your new spouse strategy described elsewhere in this book on handling verbal outbursts (tantrums). Even if your new spouse insists that the kids really hate him or her, resist that argument. Resist asking the kids to be polite or try very hard to like the new spouse. The person who should be trying *is not your kids, but the new spouse. He or she must recognize the normalcy of the kids' reactions.*

Problem 10. Pressure on your children to listen to you, not your new spouse. Funny loyalties develop where your kids only behave good around you but are ghastly and disrespectful around your new spouse.

Solution: First, make sure you and your new spouse use consistent discipline. Second, have your new spouse apply strategies in your presence so your kids will listen to him or her with you around. Third, reward the kids for their compliance to your new spouse.

The hardest job in starting a stepfamily, in other words, is trying to get on with your life without the kids feeling like they are left behind in the previous marriage. But they can be part of the new marriage if you let them. They need to see how this new marriage benefits them as much as it does you. But take it slowly. Let the experience gradually fade into focus as the kids share in this important transition.

CHAPTER 8

Should Your Child Go To Daycare?

"Wake up, kids, it's time for school!" Every morning it's the same thing. Wake up at 5 a.m. Stumble in the darkness into each child's room. Awaken them from a deep sleep. Plead, argue, do whatever you can until they get dressed. But get dress quickly. Then you race back to your room to get dressed. Last minute details always forgotten. Speed through breakfast to leave the house by 7 a.m. And barely make it on time.

And for what? Why the stress? Are today's parents really inborn Type A personalities? Powerhouse energy in the morning to get off to a roaring start? No, not at all. How about the obvious. Everybody *must* be on time. On the road by 7 a.m to miss the traffic. Be at work by 8 a.m. And drop the kids off at daycare. What's that, your kids go where? A *daycare*? That's right, daycare. It's the real thing.

What is daycare anyway? So much controversy surrounds day care today that caring parents really don't know what to do. Working parents face even tougher decisions. If I put my child in daycare from 7 a.m. to 6 p.m., that makes a career possible. And that's half the nation's 6.1 million mothers of infants and toddlers at work. We're talking lots of people. But that also limits how much time kids spend at home getting to know mom and dad. It's a tough decision, all right. Think of the worst scenario for a moment: Suppose no day care. Kids stay at home all day until they are ready for kindergarten. That means one parent— Mom or Dad—gets elected to babysit. Is that a better alternative? Hmm. It's a toss up.

In today's career–advancing fervor, it's unlikely either mom or dad really want the babysitting job. Working parents striving ahead for better jobs, higher wages, status, and independence resist being homebound. That leaves kids no choice but going to day care. But how good is it for them? Does research advise against it? Or does the yellow light say "go with caution?" Answers to these tough questions are worth considering. Let's start by asking, "Why is day care bad?" Then ask, "Why is day care good?" Then, "Why there are no straight answers ." The section after that hits the nail right on the head with why parents who have their children in daycare feel wrong—it is because they feel lonely. Finally, how to resolve the lonely trap and steps to find a safe daycare.

Why Is Daycare Bad?

How long do your kids spend at day care? Twelve hours? Maybe more? A hug, kiss, and wave of farewell at 7 a.m. is the last contact they have with you until you pick them up at 6 p.m? Is this your child? Less than 18 months old, who are left in day care 20 hours a week or more? If so, that's very normal. But that's also considerable time away from home, from you, from parents. Traditionally home means *nurturing*. Kids receive personal attention, play games and build bonds of solid parent–child relationships. Happiness from emotional caretaking strengthens a child's self–esteem and correct perception of the world around him. Do these things diminish if children go to day care?

Child specialist Jay Belsky believes this happens. Belsky, a Pennsylvania State University psychologist who has followed the research for 10 years, leads the challenge against daycare. He says infants at daycare run risks of emotional insecurity and becoming socially backward. In 1977, when Professor Belsky first examined daycares, he found little negative effects. But in recent years his tune has changed. He now says daycare undermines a child's sense of trust, including the stress a child undergoes as a result of daily separation from the mother. That children receive insufficient attention from parents when they spend a large amount of time in daycare.

Besides lacking attention, Belsky argues the children are more demanding, disobedient, aggressive, bratty, bossy, and down right unpleasant. But compared to who? Belsky has an answer. Says Belsky, compared to children who stay at home. Belsky bases his findings on two sources. First is psychologist Ainsworth's famous experiment of the "Strange Situation." This is where a child first plays with a stranger's toys left alone in a room with a stranger. That woman plays with and comforts the child while the mother is absent. The mother then returns for her child, faced with any number of infant reactions. First is a child embracing the mother; second is a child ignoring the mother, and a host of variations in between.

Claims Ainsworth, this signifies good versus bad parent–child attachment. Children who approach the returning parent after time apart are emotionally secure. But infants who avoid physical contact or who spend little time with returning parents are insecure. This "Strange Situation" exposes how much trust and assurance children have toward themselves and parents. Anxious children get scared right from the start and may be suspicious of that stranger. Secure children play right away with toys, greeting the stranger. But the key fact here is "time apart." Theorists say extended periods of separation between child and parent could disrupt and diminish that child's sense of physical and emotional response to caregivers. This eventually undermines the parent's nurturing and authority role and breaks the bond of parent–child trust.

Sounds pretty scary, huh? Belsky and his associates further warn that after daycare, things may get worse. Insecurely attached children grow up with fears, feel incompetent, and have poor self–control. Toddlers and preschoolers shows less sympathy, are less compliant, and are loners. This leads to the second source of data. Research besides the "Strange Situation," on preschool and grown-up children, again showed this insecure–avoidant nature and poor attachment. In studies from 1982 and 1984, preschool children judged insecure also were more anxious, aggressive, and hyperactive than their peers. Another study, of middle–class children, found that those who had begun daycare before turning 18 months old were more prone to cry and misbehave at ages nine and ten. But infants whose mothers returned to work on a full–time basis prior to the infant's 6–month birthday may or may not be insecure—it all depended. On what? On the timing of the child's entry into day care.

In other words, critics of day care argue that time apart and early entry to daycare threaten the infant's proper development. That removal of caregivers deprives children of emotional needs and literally destroys the infant–mother attachment bond. Sounds like "fight'n words." Pretty high stakes for the sake of a career, wouldn't you say? It's enough to shame any parent into years of guilt— unless of course, there's something wrong with the research. Is the research on children *really valid?*

You see, that's the problem with research. Not all research is valid research. So much of what people read about looks like research but really is just concocted guesses or thrown–together surveys. Did you read, lately, that most women 42 years and older prefer dating younger men than older men? It appeared all over the tabloids. Survey reports tallied this finding but the *method* of doing the survey was invalid. And so the results, no matter how sensational sounding they were, must be taken with a grain of salt.

Results from the "Strange Situation" can also be taken with a grain of salt if you consider a few points. First, this study really was unfair. Situations were set up for children living at home, not for children already at day care. Second, what about a child who avoids his mother when she returns in the playroom. Studies says this is abnormal. But is there another way to look at *avoidance behavior*? How about this: that preschoolers who avoid their parents really are being *independent*. True independence may mean infants play alone or without needing a caretaker's emotional assurance.

Third, how much time apart is a *long* time apart? Research does not address infants spending one day at daycare versus extensive daycare experience. Is there really any difference between a child going to daycare one to two days a week versus ones who are there full–time? Fourth, different things these children do in this "Strange Situation" might also account for their behaviors. Suppose infants are hurt playing with a sharp toy or get angry because the toy is defective or wrong for make–believe. Anger can transfer from play to the returning parent. This anger would have nothing to do with being at daycare or always at home. What *caused* the anger would be the toy, not the child's immaturity, aggressiveness, or hyperactivity.

Belsky, Ainsworth and other child specialists still feel that nonmaternal care is bad for kids. But Belsky offers another idea: What if it's not the daycare that is the problem, but rather the home life of children who have nonmaternal care. So, being at daycare may be okay, but what little time children spend with mom and dad is *really what should be looked at*. And so the debate goes on.

Why Is Day Care Good?

Turning the argument around and looking at homelife is the first valid step. Psychologist Clarke–Stewart also says things begin at home, and that the "Strange Situation" is no measure of emotional security. Let's consider this thing— "security" anyway. What is it? Security is not a personality trait. Nobody really is "insecure." It's not part of the brain. You can't find it next to the temporal lobe. So what is it? Security is a *relationship*. What infants have are secure and insecure relationships with people around them. And the best yardstick of a secure relationships is *how adaptable children are*. Do daycare children adapt to strange new situations pretty well? Yes, they do.

Take the behaviors Belsky said would ruin an infant. That a child becomes stubborn, selfish, demanding, noncompliant and possibly aggressive. Now think of exactly what this means for *adaptive* children. *Stubborn* children are independent— want to do things themselves. *Demanding* children are assertive and creative. *Noncompliant* children think for themselves and possibly resist an adult's arbitrary rules made only so adults can remain in control. And *aggressive*? Any time independent children or adults are belittled or forced into subservience, they rebel. Aggression results.

Let's put it to a further test. Ask yourself. Do I want a shy, passively dependent child? Or will my child be a leader? Supporters of day care say that early entry into school really stimulates thinking, creativity, and builds important socialization skills. That's how later adult assertiveness emerges. This does not mean early daycare infants are insensitive to feelings or grow up hating their parents. It only means they are more vocal, more specific, and perhaps develop different attachments to mom and dad. In fact, it is clear from Belsky's own summary figures that over half the infants in full–time daycare show secure attachment.

The red flags against daycare are waving stronger than they need to be. Research doesn't support it. Frightening hard–working parents at a time when two–family incomes are necessary, and daycares are the best alternative, is like saying you shouldn't use gasoline in your car. It creates air pollutants damaging the atmosphere. But you have to use gas because you have to have a car. It's that simple. The same is true for daycare.

The jury is still out on the verdict of daycares and possibly will remain undecided for a long time. Answers probably will not be known until preschoolers grow up and raise children of their own. So, in the meantime, use resources wisely. For some kids, it's probably exactly the right thing. And for other kids, daycare may not be the right thing. Here's how to figure it out.

Why There Are No Straight Answers

Working parents really want to work. Or they have to work. So, first consider a few things. If bratty children really are assertive children. And, if my infant who avoids me really is being independent. Then maybe daycare promotes faster emotional growth than moms and dads can provide through regular home–nurturing.

As for fears of having "bad children." New research points out some other reasons why children turn out good and bad. First, of course, are the many daycare factors, from teacher's personality to program curricula. Second are factors about your child himself. Even before entering day care, is he shy, or very talkative? Third factors are family lifestyle. Never underestimate this. Parents giving a lot of positive attention and rewards for behavior, using guidance and compassion, generally raise children who are independent whether the kids go to daycare or stay at home. Whereas parents using much negative discipline and upset by daily negative behaviors at home may find their infants more noncompliant or aggressive no matter where the children are.

Choosing the best option for your child depends, then, on two factors. *First* is your own personal preference on how you want your children to behave. *Second* is how much *you* need their constant dependence on you. Career mothers can wear both hats, worker and parent, if they let their infants be stronger, more assertive, and need less attachment. This may sound hard, especially if you like being hugged and kissed after a long hard work day. And all you get instead is a cold shoulder from your child. Assertive, direct and expressive children get ahead faster, are more reliable, and still can enjoy the experiences of childhood. If you want a child who *needs you*, then you're setting your child up for dependency. He cries for you. She asks permission from you on everything before she does it. Is that your preference?

The danger with children *who depend on their parents is that they are afraid to act on their own.* They never get that chance to be on their own, exploring curiosities of the world, for fear of being told they are bad for doing it. Jack picks up his father's ledger from work and flips through the pages. His father swoops it out of his hand and spanks him for getting into dad's things. *Bad Jack. He tried being curious and got punished for it.* Now Jack stays away not from his dad's belongings, but also from all new toys or objects—even the ones he *is supposed to touch and explore.*

Dependency on parents develops for another reason. It has more to do with parents than children. Moms, especially, may agree with Belsky's bad attitude about daycare so that she can have company. You see, it's too lonely staying home alone, not working, and feeling unloved. What's a mother to do?

Do You Feel Lonely?

It's a real feeling to look around an empty house and say, "nobody cares about me. What value am I to anybody?" Put your fears to the test by looking at the statements below. Which of these statements do you believe are true?

1.   I am unhappy doing so many things alone.
2.   I have nobody to talk to.
3.   I cannot tolerate being so alone.
4.   I feel as if nobody really understands me.
5.   I find myself waiting for people to call or write.
6.   I feel completely alone.

7.   I am unable to reach out and communicate with those around me.

8.   I feel starved for company.

9.   I feel starved for affection.

10.   I feel starved for attention.

11.   It is difficult for me to make friends.

12.   I feel shut out and excluded by others.

(Adapted from "UCLA Loneliness Scale" from *Developing a measure of loneliness* by D. Russell, L.A. Peplau and M.L. Ferguson *Journal of Personality Assessment*, 1978, 42, 290–294.)

"Yes" to most or all of them means your lonely index is very high. That desperately needed is time with friends, your spouse, family or special adult people, instead of filling the void entirely with your children. Becoming this lonely does not happen overnight. It's not a new feeling. Slowly, gradually, your sense of isolation builds from a mild emptiness to moderate loneliness; you stay home more, you visit less people, and still fewer visit you at your house. And finally it hits: detachment from the world scares you into thinking that nobody cares for who you are, what you do, and why you exist.

Why Loneliness Occurs

Loneliness creeps into your life piece by piece, just when you think things are going great. Finally you have a job—or have stopped working. Spouse is at work. Ahead of you are endless hours spent the way you always wanted them. Organized, productive, and individualized. Little stands in your way now that the kids are at daycare or in school full–time. Nothing should interrupt your active flow of 4 to 5 scheduled hours taking you to every distant corner of town. Nothing will ruin it, except your deeply swelling sensation of unhappiness. That the kids or *somebody* is not there tagging along or building your confidence. It makes everyday so boring.

But why does this happen? How do you accidentally let the virus of loneliness enter into the body and break down all sensible immune systems? The answers lies with seven main reasons why all people feel lonely:

1.   Fear of conflict
2.   Fear of rejection
3.   Fear of vulnerability
4.   Fear of adjustment
5.   Fear of positive attention
6.   Fear of intimacy and homophobia

7.   Fear of risks

Fear of conflict.   The worst thing in the world, so it seems, is facing people who disagree with me or who offend me. What do I say? This fear instills utter panic in parents who refuse to upset people or say "no." Refusals might set off a person who yells, screams, argues, or scares you. And the scariest part is not knowing how to respond back. Parents avoid conflict by simply staying at home, or limiting shopping trips or outings to times of day when contact with masses of people is infrequent or unlikely.

Fear of rejection. Those same people who confront me also hate me. *I know they hate me because they criticize, hurt my feelings, and make me hate myself.* Rejection stabs like a knife right where it hurts—right in the gut of sensitivity. What people say, how they say it or assumptions you make cause deadly fears about being disapproved by other people. Parents avoid rejection by selecting contact only with people who they can control or make them feel good. All others are put out of sight, out of mind.

Fear of vulnerability. Fear of conflict, of rejection stem from not wanting to look stupid.

Horrible panic sets in when you think people perceive you as dumb, idiotic or not knowing what you're talking about. That loss of control is so humiliating that parents refuse to let it happen. Places or people around whom you feel scared, not in control, or may look incompetent are avoided at all costs.

Fear of adjustment. This goes hand in hand with fear of vulnerability. Not only is looking stupid bad, but "How could I look stupid in a new situation?" Parents may bypass new shops, stores, cities, malls, or anything not familiar to them because it means an adjustment. Adjustment entails talking to strangers (contact and confrontation), asking directions (looking stupid), and relying on yourself to get around (being out of control or vulnerable). Instead, shopping restricts you to safe, easily accessible and familiar places.

Fear of positive attention. This may seem unusual but it is all too common among parents who grew up embarrassed all the time. *I hate receiving compliments and always feel like people are lying.* Being in the world means contact with people who say good things, as well as bad things to you. But if compliments send intense chills up and down your vertebrae, it means you distrust these comments and feel compelled to disqualify them. Saying things like, "Oh, thank you, but really it's nothing," or "it's not really a nice dress, considering I bought it at the Salvation Army." Down–playing your attire, your physical body, or anything about yourself means you hate to draw attention to yourself for fear that people might perceive you as arrogant, a braggart, or selfish. Not boasting means being humble. And parents who humbly make excuses when giving a compliment also are hesitant to be around complimentary (good) people.

Fear of intimacy and homophobia. How close can you get to a friend? Lonely parents who seek close friends risk exposure of their personality or faults to these people. It becomes awkward. *What will they think of me?* Close contact deepens the sharing experience. Secrets and true confessions are disclosed—but at what price? Hopefully at the price of keeping those secrets confidential. But even getting to that point of disclosure can be an anxious experience. Anxiety doubles when men or women distrust this friend–to–be for sexual reasons. Not heterosexual reasons, but homosexual reasons. Particularly for parents who find it suspicious when people treat them nicely, they might mistaken friendly gestures and warmth as a "come–on" from the same–sex friend. *She can't possibly be this nice unless she has something up her sleeve—she wants something...I know that for sure. She definitely wants something.* Distrust forbids close friendships because of thinking that person wants a homosexual relationship.

Fear of risks.   Bottom–line. Parents are afraid of trying new things. And *newness* can be anything. New friends, new places, new foods, new hobbies, new everything.   Risk means subjecting yourself to the same tortuous fears of rejection and conflict, that it is too overwhelming to do. Parents imprisoned by fear of risk surround their lives with simple, safe, and controllable tasks and do not step outside this boundary even if they know it is best for them to do so.

How To Beat the Lonely Trap and Find the Best Daycare

So now you're stuck on the horns of a dilemma. On the one hand daycare is okay and you're willing to have your kids go there. But an empty house gets awfully lonely. You get this thick lump in your throat every time you think of not seeing the kids for 5 or 8 hours after your drop them off. What's the best thing to do?

First, get rid of that loneliness on your own before the kids become the solution. Second, sketch out a strategy on evaluating exactly what a good daycare should have in it. Let's take care of loneliness first.

No More Loneliness

Erasing loneliness is no easy task. It means stepping outside that warm, insulated comfort zone into a dark unknown where people judge you, disapprove of you, and dislike you. It means risking opinions, and opening up yourself to situations you may later regret. Breaking out of the loneliness trap especially means finding your own niche in life either in a career or activity that is personally rewarding and gives you confidence. It means creating and enjoying leisure time. How do you begin doing this? Well, ask yourself, what do I like to do? Who do I like to do it with? How do I want to do it? These are factors that contribute to your leisure activity. Figure out these factors by going through an inventory such as the one below:

Inventory of Leisure Needs

Rank in order of preference, the three best choices to each of the following questions. A "1" indicates the most preferred, "2" the next most preferred, and so on.

1.   How many people do you prefer being with during your leisure?

_ _   Alone

_ _   With one person

_ _   With a small group (3–5)

_ _   With a medium–sized group (6–12)

_ _   With a large group (13 or more)

2.   What age–group do you prefer being with during your leisure?

_ _   Your same age

_ _   Younger than you

_ _   Older than you

_ _   No preference

3.   Which people do you prefer your leisure time with?

_ _   Spouse

_ _   Spouse and children

_ _   Friend(s)

_ _   Family (other than spouse and children)

_ _   Stranger(s)

4.   With which sex do you prefer to spend your leisure?

_ _   Male(s)

_ _   Female(s)

_ _   Both sexes

5.   What is the marital status of people you prefer to spend your leisure?

_ _   Single individuals

_ _   Married individuals

_ _   Both married and single individuals

_ _   Single couples

_ _   Married couples

_ _   Both married and single couples

6.   What nature do you prefer your leisure activity to involve?

_ _   Physical

_ _   Intellectual

_ _   Social

_ _   Emotional

_ _   Creative

7.   Which of the following do you prefer in your leisure?

_ _   Mental stimulation

_ _   Interaction with people

_ _   Physical exertion

_ _   Skill requirement

_ _   Obvious results

_ _   Involvement as a spectator

_ _   Other (specify) _____

8.   What feelings do you prefer to receive from your leisure?

    _ _   Feeling of achievement
    _ _   Feeling of pleasure
    _ _   Feeling of satisfaction
    _ _   Feeling of relaxation
    _ _   Feeling of self–worth
    _ _   Feeling of recognition
    _ _   Other (specify) _____

9.   In what environment do you prefer to spend your leisure?

    _ _   Indoors or around the home
    _ _   In a city or town
    _ _   By a body of water
    _ _   In the mountains
    _ _   In the forest

10.   How familiar should the place be where you spend leisure?

    _ _   In an unknown place
    _ _   In a place similar to other places you've been
    _ _   In a place you've been before

11.   What kind of climate do you prefer for your leisure?

    _ _   Hot
    _ _   Moderate

_ _   Cold

12.   During what time of day do you prefer your leisure?

    _ _   Morning

    _ _   Afternoon

    _ _   Evening

13.   How do you prefer your leisure to be structured?

    _ _   A lot of rules and regulations

    _ _   Some rules and regulations

    _ _   No rules and regulations

14.   How many activities do you wish to do for leisure?

    _ _   One activity

    _ _   A few activities (3–5)

    _ _   Many activities (6 or more)

15.   In activities involving skills, do you prefer to be with people who are:

    _ _   Of greater skill level than you

    _ _   Of less skill level than you

    _ _   Of equal skill level

16.   Which do you prefer in your leisure activities?

    _ _   No competition

    _ _   A little competition

    _ _   Lots of competition

17.   How much do you want to participate in your leisure?

   _ _   To be a spectator
   _ _   To be an occasional spectator
   _ _   To be an active participant

18.   How long should the projects be in your leisure?

   _ _   Short term (can complete in a few hours)
   _ _   Medium (can complete in a few days)
   _ _   Long term (requires a week or longer to complete)

19.   Do you prefer activities that require a leader?

   _ _   No
   _ _   Yes (if "yes," please continue with the last two questions)

20.   What age leader do you prefer in your leisure?

   _ _   Near your age
   _ _   Older
   _ _   Younger

21.   Would you prefer your leader to be?

   _ _   A friend
   _ _   An acquaintance
   _ _   A stranger

(Source: Adapted from Fandozzi, R., Knight, K.M. & Sutton, C. (1979). Worksheet 14: Inventory of preferred leisure factors and conditions. In J. Mundy & L. Odum (Eds.). *Leisure education: Theory and practice*. NY: John Wiley.)

Now that you know what you like, dislike and will try for leisure activities, you are ready to dismantle old habits of loneliness. Do this by:

1.   *Observing your behavior*. Watch how you communicate and try specific methods on speaking clearly, directly, and not worrying about how it sounds.

2.   *Volunteering in groups and organizations*. Participate in local, religious, and special groups having your similar interests. Join a committee, a school, or religious school council, or human service agency. For example, hospitals welcome volunteers who can offer 2 to 5 hours weekly.

3.   *Becoming outgoing and visible*. No matter where you volunteer or are active, especially among groups of 3 or more, be expressive and draw attention to yourself. At first, self–attention feels mechanical, forced—even phoney, as if all around

you see right through your facade. But they don't. Not because people are blind, but because you really are not phony. It just feels that way.

4. *Role–playing new behaviors.* Don't knock it until you try it. Surprisingly, assuming the role of a person you admire can muster bravery when you feel like a chicken. Think about who you know that is assertive, risk–taking, and shrugs off insults. Act out this person's verbal characteristics or even physical movements long enough to overcome initial butterflies. Once comfortable, shift roles from this vicarious person to yourself. The idea, in other words, is not to lose yourself invisibly in another personality, but to borrow that personality as a springboard for your own skill–building.

5. *Increasing your daily schedule.* Plot a path of busy activities during the prime time of your day. Go to new places, with new people, staying longer than before. Old warning signs of fear will still trigger when you get scared or feel strange pretending you're enjoying yourself when you really may not be. But ignore them. Resist compulsive thoughts lying to you about how you really "should return home," that "what your

doing is too risky," and that "if you get too busy something bad might happen." Put this pessimism out to pasture.

6.   *Relaxing your body.* Recall in Chapter 6 methods of relaxation that put your body at immediate ease. Use these procedures to release stiff muscles before the tension frightens you back into old habits of avoidance and escape.

7.   *Stopping your wrong thoughts.* Earlier chapters also discussed the deadly cycle of personalizing things people do. Prevent this trap by sticking with the facts of the situation and focusing only on what is going on. Temptation will draw you into worrying about everything, but resist it. If obsessive thoughts get out of control, focus on objects around you or on what the person is saying to you. Ask questions, contribute to the conversation, but do not remain silent.

8.   *Telling people about your changes.* Sounds like bragging, again, doesn't it? Well, it sounds like bragging because it is bragging. But verbalizing about how you've beat the loneliness trap serves another function. Words you say aloud to listeners

very quickly turn into personal thoughts you carry around with you. If you deliberately discuss how you went to new places, that you kept busy while the kids were at daycare, and how rewarding the experience was, within a week you will be thinking these same verbal statements. They become ego–boosting thoughts after you broadcast them in front of a live audience.

These strategies move you rapidly in the direction of confidence and remove loneliness. They also afford you risk–taking habits that you previously denied or felt were dangerous. The danger, of course, is now gone. You are alive with renewed adult interest and motivated to keep up the energetic pace just as long as you can find a safe daycare.

Choosing the Best Daycare

Finding the right daycare is a tough job. Flipping through pages of yellow–page ads or sorting through tips and leads from friends and family goes on and on forever. It never stops—until you *have to find a daycare or else be stuck without one.* Desperate means may call for desperate action of starting with one daycare or careprovider you are unsatisfied with. That's not a good idea. It turns into a mess before you know it. Is there a better way of going at this impossible mission? Yes. there is.

Which daycare or caregiver you explore is really only the beginning. The name can come out of the yellow pages or by word of mouth or by shopping around for the best weekly rates. Many jobs now even subscribe to a child–care referral system on computer. In the human resource or personnel office may be a computer hooked up to an on–line child–care (CCARE) database through the Human Resource Information Network (HRIN). HRIN is an on–line retrieval service for personnel professionals. CCARE provides working parents with a list of licensed full–day and part–day child–care centers and homes in their area. The nationwide listings supplies more than 50 items of information, including years of experience, handicapped capabilities and times, dates of need. Again, this on–line database is available if your personnel office subscribes to HRIN.

So, choosing a daycare or caregiver is the first step. Now, how do you figure out if it *really does what it says it does?* Even trusting parents optimistic about daycare, are careful to screen out good from bad places. But based on what? The best way of screening people and places is a having a *criteria*. Jot down a list of important features expected in a daycare or its providers you would want for your child. Be generous with your list and expand it as your needs direct you. Two types of daycare you probably will judge are *daycare centers* and *family day care*. Daycare centers hold large numbers of children in school–like settings. Family daycare are when infants or children are cared for in small groups or in someone else's home.

In both cases, ask yourself similar questions to determine if the place or person you have in mind passes your test of criteria. Here are common questions to ask:

1.   *What is the teacher/child ratio?*
In general, the lower the better, although one national study shows that within the range of 5:1 to 10:1 it doesn't matter much. Ratios of 15:1 and higher are not advised.

2.   *How many children are there per group?*
Regardless of how many adults there are with each group of children, it is always best to have a small number of children cared for together. Thus a group of 30 children cared for by 5 adults is not as

good as three smaller groups of 10 children cared for by 1 adult each.

3.   *How much personal contact does your child have with the caregiver?*

The more time your child spends with adult attention, the better it is for growth. Number of hours, minutes and seconds are less important than overall attention being paid to your child's needs or stimulating his or her creativity.

4.   *How much verbal stimulation should your child receive?*

A lot. No matter how many toys are available, it does not replace the diversity and warmth of words adults use to describe your child. Caregivers who are descriptive, take time for details and answer questions, stimulate faster language and cognitive development.

5.   *How spacious, clean and colorful should the daycare be?*

The physical organization of space makes a difference. Your child will show more creative play in colorful, clean environments that are laid out for child's play. Lots of toys around, with mats or bright colors on walls and pictures is very enriching. Expensive toys are not critical, and in fact may inhibit imagination. There should also be enough space for children to move around freely.

6. *How knowledgeable should caregivers be about child development?*

That's a good question. And the opinion on it is mixed. Many fine quality daycare centers through churches and synagogues or in a person's home may lack trained child experts. Experts as far as receiving college training or being a licensed teacher. Rare exceptions are schools offering daycare *and* private school that only hire licensed caregivers. The safe bet is placing your child with *either* (a) experienced caregivers with a smart and spotless reputation, or (b) caregivers who are licensed teachers or earned degrees or certification in childcare or child development.

7. *Should the caregiver be married or single?*

Sounds biased, but true. Family daycare providers who are single are responsible for all the care of the home as well as the children. They may spend more time in housekeeping and less time with children than do married caregivers.

8.   *What is the make–up of kids?*

Let's move a little deeper with bias, shall we? Parents may be firm on not mixing their children with different races, ethnic groups or religious groups. Daycare centers or homes tailoring only to one religion, say, Catholic or Jewish, are sought out. And they are not hard to find if a parent gets leads along the friendship grapevine. But is that really the *best* type of daycare? No, it is not. The more integrated the composition of boys and girls—from all backgrounds—the more it stimulates growth.

9.   *What are the goals of the program?*

Is the emphasis *entirely* on playtime? Or is there dual emphasis on playtime and academics. Daycare for infants shy away from academic curricula, believing that school work presented too early might spoil a child's healthy curiosity and imagination. But research shows just the opposite. Planned activities that have an educational flavor along with fun and games can speed learning at an earlier age. Be sure the teachers or caregivers offer some academics in the form or reading, writing, coloring, or exposure to arts and sciences.

10. *What is the organization of the classroom or home?*

Just because daycare takes on some school features does not mean it must be run like a military school. Inflexibility is dangerous to eager learning. Be sure teachers or caregivers are flexible with time, activities, and even scheduled lesson plans. Learning should be a fun experience, not a college prep class.

11. *How is discipline used?*

First, is it used at all? And if so, what type of discipline? Is the emphasis leaning more positive or negative? Are rewards used? And for what? Questions like these pinpoint exactly how teachers or caregiver will handle your child's misbehavior. This is especially important after all the time and effort you spent improving your child's behavior. The last thing you want to happen is seeing this progress deteriorate at the sloppy hands of negative teachers. Try to coordinate your efforts with the teacher or caregiver. Explain what you do, why you do it, and ask for daily or weekly reports (2–minute chats when you pick up your child at the end of the day).

Working together with daycare providers is absolutely necessary to prevent problems. It is all too common to have a child pretty as a picture at home and wreaking havoc at school. Personality splits happen when you keep your end of the bargain—using the behavior strategies—but teachers and caregivers slip back into old habits. This gives attention to your child who *only recently stopped acting out for attention.* Green lights go back on for this attention and your child acts out just like before, *but only where attention is available.* That is why it stuns you to hear your precious, polite child who has been angel at home and is driving the staff crazy. Now you know: It may be the staff who are driving the child crazy. But it pays to first check out what is going on.

12. *How is praise used?*

Every caregiver, teacher and daycare owner agrees with the motto that high doses of praise strengthens good behavior. That's not up for debate. What *is up for debate is how praise is given.* Do providers give strokes only when good behavior is done? When it is visible? Or when the child finally behaves nicely after being a tyrant? The rule of thumb is this: *Praise needs to occur as much and for as many behaviors as possible.* Don't let providers wait until the right time to reward children with praise. Let them do it now, anytime, for any reason. (The only exception is to withhold praise and rewards if your child's behavior is inappropriate. Consult the chapter on tantrums for a reminder.)

13. *What responsibilities do your children have?* Daycare is typically an adult world. Games, toys, activities and all events revolve around the teacher's or caregiver's schedule. And there is nothing wrong with this. But does your child have any input on decisions? Can she choose which toys or games to play with? Can your child be a leader or play "adult" roles? They should. Make sure your child has "free–play; it builds proper problem–solving skills. Your child should also have many chances to be leader in the group or teacher's helper.

Following these "criteria" is a good start. It means you are consciousness about the welfare of your child and his early education. It also means you took the time and energy to say, "who else besides myself can raise my child according to my standards?" And there's nothing harder than releasing your own protective shield from around your child. It hurts and even gets scary. But that's all part of returning a life to yourself so you can prosper in feeling alive and productive.

CHAPTER 9

When Does Your Child Need Therapy?

Melissa tantrums uncontrollably at school and home.

Bruce swears at his teachers and says "so what."

Billy hits his mother and father all the time. Sandra is so anxious that anything bothers her.

Is this "normal" behavior? Some say, "Well, it depends on the situation." Take Melissa, for example. It depends on whether her parents yelled at her first or are giving attention to tantrums. Take Craig—swearing and not caring. He's immune to what people think. Did somebody teach him to do that? Who eggs him on? Even those who say Bruce is a "psychopath" admit he leaves people alone until pushed. So, if so many people make excuses for him, why say he's a psychopath? He must be normal.

Decisions on what is and is not normal determine whether therapy is sought. Melissa, Bruce, Billy, Sandra—all of them in one way or another act on the surface like nothing is wrong. Perhaps there is nothing wrong. At least, some people around them find nothing wrong with their behavior. Nothing, that is, by whatever definition of normality or sanity these people believe in.

The definition does make a difference. This chapter first explains why "normal" is a tricky term and determines when children need therapy. Some odd beliefs about normalcy get in the way of a good definition and these will also have to be explained. Also, if being "abnormal" is not the answer, then what is? What tell–tale signs really cue parents in on the way children behave, and whether the need for therapy exists?

Who Says Behavior Is Wrong?

Good question. Many people say it's wrong. Parents say it's wrong. Teachers say it's wrong. And a host of trusting professionals may agree. But there are usually good reasons why outsiders consider a child's behavior a problem. Here are three of the most popular ones:

1.   The behavior is new, different and unlike anything your child has done before.

2.   The behavior seems out of place. It's normal, but happening at the wrong time for the wrong reasons.

3.   The behavior is different from how other children or *you (the parent)* might behave under similar situations.

Behavior is New or Different

Child development is somewhat predictable. Physical changes are obvious. Changes in speech, language and overall communication are also visible to the eye and most parents expect these things. But what about the subtle changes in personality? Children who typically react in one way, and have done so for 2 to 3 years seem like they are forming a pattern. "Well, that's the way Beth will probably always handle stress." Today's childhood actions lay the foundations for tomorrow's young adult. At least that is the intuitive belief.

But personality or behavioral development takes many left and right turns that are not on the map. When this happens, and parents wonder what's gotten into their son or daughter, the verdict is usually negative. Parents presume their child has a problem. Harold, for example, says "thank you" all the time—very polite around adults. Today he didn't. Not just once, twice or three times, but all day. And that's not all. He also sneered at each adult asking him how he was—"none of your business," he shouted back. Needless to say, his parents concluded, "that's definitely not our Harold." Well, then, who is he?

It's Harold all right. And changes in his behavior flash red lights all over the intersection so that his parents believe there is a problem. Is it a problem or is Harold entitled to experience normal mood swings of being sweet and being devilish all in the same day?

Behavior Seems Out of Place

The story is different for Amanda. Her parents are accustomed to her backtalking and being rude around other people. She loves attention and seizes it from any adults who show interest in her. It annoys her parents and both of them recently started using strategies to change their daughter's tantruming. So, they didn't expect what happened. Amanda went with her parents to the grocery store Saturday afternoon when it was filled with kids and adults. Strategy or no strategy, her parents were expecting the worse. But there was a strange twist in behavior. Amanda stood next to her parents and the shopping cart the whole time. When introduced to other families, she politely responded and used formal words like "nice to meet you," and "have a good day."

Her behavior was very unusual and very suspicious. Her parents did not know what to make of it. So they concluded the obvious: It must be a fluke since *her behavior is out of place*. It's too good to be true and probably the honeymoon won't last. Her parents were certain Amanda's good behavior was strange and especially for being in the grocery store. But really, now. Was it?

Behavior is Different from How You or Others Behave

What if your child does something so good or so bad but you can't make sense of it because nobody else behaves this way? Surely, *you wouldn't behave this way were you in your child's situation.* When actions deviate from the norm, that's a dead give–away the behavior will be called abnormal. Fifteen year old Fred knew it was winter. He had eyes; he saw the snow outside and felt the 20 degree temperature with ice under his feet. But it didn't matter. He insisted on wearing his Addidas gym shoes without socks. No way, no socks. This astonished his parents and they thought he's lost all contact with reality. "How preposterous?" "He'll freeze to death!"

Gym shoes without socks were the popular thing to do and Fred knew it. Some kids dressed this way and others did not. But because this attire so radically violated a dress code, and especially for the season, Fred's actions were up for prosecution. But was he really a deviant child?

The eye of the perceiver is what counts. Who perceives the behavior and says it is inappropriate depends on *where they are, what's going on at the time, and the history of that person with the child.*

Let's consider perceptions from the most common adults who come in contact with your child.

Parents

    Parents form opinions from day to day contact based on several factors. Age, physical health, compliance, noncompliance, friendship and love for their children. A parent's eyes are deeply rooted in the lifestyle, needs and idiosyncrasies of that child. When so engulfed in the flames, it's difficult to realize you're burning. That is why you may not catch certain habits or patterns developing that are abnormal or could lead to troubled times.

Friends

    Friends are an unusual breed. Spectators in part, and yet more deeply entrenched in the day–to–day feelings, thoughts and goals of your children just by spending more time with them. On the school bus, in classrooms, after school, on the phone at night, and then on the weekends. Friends occupy a central, sometimes monopolizing role in child development that doubles in intensity around adolescence. Then it is nearly impossible to separate your precious offspring from the tightly pulling clutches of peer groups.

So friends have some leverage on the matter of how your children behave. If told by a friend that your child is not eating and looks anorexic, perhaps there is some truth to it—even if your child looks physically fine. Then, too, where there is leverage, leverage can be used improperly to spoil friendships or sabotage peer groups, especially if friendship is between a boy and girl. Your daughter's best friend squeals on her about what she *may be doing with a guy sexually.* Rather than panic, ask yourself if the informant also wants that boyfriend.

Grandparents

There is a prerequisite to saying a child's behavior is abnormal. The person has to really *care about that child.* And that's exactly how grandparents feel about their grandchildren. They love them dearly with the greatest admiration for their emotional welfare. Aunts and uncles also feel this way and show it in compliments or by pulling you aside for negative comments. But grandparents take the Oscar award for caring because they usually see the children more frequently. Honest opinions offered by your mother, father or your spouse's mother or father take authority status. Why, they should know what they're talking about, shouldn't they? They had kids and probably are more perceptive than you or your spouse, right?

Not exactly. Your parents and your spouse's parents may be right on the money on perceptions, but for different reasons. They perceive appropriate or inappropriate behavior *compared to you as a child or children raised at least 15 to twenty years ago, if not more.* Crying children, for instance, used to mean a colicky child. That meant illness and the need to show more love and attention. A loved child who feels warmth from mother or father might stop excessive crying. At least, that's how it used to be. But you know better. Once you eliminate medical reasons, you instantly know the consequence of giving more attention to a crying, possibly tantruming child. So you explain this thinking to your parents or in–laws. It appalls them—"you expect me to believe ignoring a child actually improves the behavior? Hogwash!"

So much for trying. Differences in perspective based on a parenting styles a generation ago might bias the opinion of good and bad behavior.

Teacher

You have to believe the teacher, don't you? Who else sees your child for 6 to 7 hours a day, five days a week, for nearly 10 months of the year? The one adult holding enormous clout as judge, jury and executioner of your child's educational future must have the wisdom to know when something is rotten. And so you implicitly trust teachers when they say your child does this right and *many of these things wrong.* But again, you must ask yourself, *wrong? Compared to whom?* Teachers err like other human beings and may get caught up in personality differences between your child and other children or other staff or even with themselves. Elementary school teachers are more prone to error by being in the same classroom as your child for 4 to 6 hours daily. Middle school or high school teachers at least get a breather. They see your child once, maybe twice daily and that distance earns them a stronger objective perspective.

But all teachers—elementary, middle school, high school—are still comparing your children to other students currently in class with them or in that teacher's history. Take their opinions seriously, check them out, but do not place stock in every word they say.

Principal

Principals in today's schools are without doubt the pillar of a community. Elementary, middle school or high school, they all symbolize God in your child's eyes and are the first real contact children have with a political or bureaucratic system . Principals or vice–principals also assume the unpleasant duties of discipline and of calling parents down to the school for a "conference." Not all vice–principals do this. Some deal strictly with the educational curriculum. Some deal with support staff and professional teams. But the majority get their fingers dirty in the sewage of behavior problems.

How truthful are principals? Very truthful. They present information in the clearest, perhaps least offensive manner aimed at getting down to the nitty gritty and finding solutions. There is one problem, however. Information they provide is second–hand knowledge. Students hurt by your child tell their teachers, who in turn communicate this incident to the vice–principal. That person may tell the principal verbally or in a written memo, which distills down the message to its barest essentials. Forget the bloody details—some of which were crucial to the story. By the time

Principal Jones says, "Yes, Mrs. Carmichael, your child is stealing food from the cafeteria," you're getting the watered down, abbreviated version that can sting you and leave you thinking, and thinking and thinking.

Once again, don't leave in doubt. Ask the principal if you can meet with the child, or child's parents or teachers to whom the incident was told. But get to the bottom line on what happened.

Physician

Trust in physicians is a rule. Nearly everybody subscribes to this rule because physicians handle life and death decisions and your entire biological future rests in their judgment. Experts in health, they also serve as confidant, mediator, and social worker. You confide in your physician, sometimes because he or she is the only person secretly available to you who *will protect your privacy*. Physicians also are the first to spot a physical symptom during an exam possibly brought on by emotional or behavioral problems. Overweight children are targets for poor stress control. Underweight children the same—but also may be diagnosed as neglected or hurt at home. And the list of possible diagnoses goes on.

So, when your physician and friend for 10, 20 or 30 years says, "you know, Gary, I wouldn't tell you this if I didn't think it was important," you suddenly prepare for Earth–shattering information. And you get it. He announces your child is hyperactive and may require certain medicines for conduct control. It devastates you, and you give the advice serious consideration.

But physicians, like teachers, are fallible. They make mistakes in diagnosis and may only perceive "bad behavior" through the narrow looking glass of their training and expertise. Most M.D.s are trained, for instance, to examine illness as originating from inside the body, or organically based. That doesn't mean physicians ignore bad parenting or things that happen to your child outside his body. It just means *treatment of the problem, whatever its cause, deals with changes in the body*. Medicine does just that. It changes the body chemistry creating a new balance that may or may not help your "hyperactive" child adjust to situations.

Now, whether you are a firm believer in medicine or not, the physician's advice is not always complete. Many D.O.s (Doctors of Osteopathy) share training of M.D.s and basically develop identical skills and become specialists in all major categories (e.g., pediatrics, psychiatry, etc.) And their diagnostic focus is on looking at all sides of the problem, not just the internal or organic side. Differences in diagnoses between M.D. physicians and D.O. physicians sometimes are astounding. Regardless of who is right, both M.D.s and D.O.s suffer a limited view of your child by only knowing about internal problems. That information is a good beginning and deserves more input from other specialists.

Psychologist/Social Worker

Psychologists are many types. So are social workers. Psychologists working with the school are "school psychologists." They specialize in testing a child for academic skills and whether outside or special services would help boost performance. Some psychologists are support staff and consult teachers with "at–risk" students who misbehave or are slow academically. Consultants design a behavioral program for teacher and student to work on together. Other psychologists are "clinical psychologists." These are specialists who may also be consultants but who see yourself or your child for "therapy." Clinical psychologists trained especially for children (pediatric psychologists) are attentive to family problems or common aggravations along the path of child development.

Social workers, like clinical psychologists, also have specialities. Some directly work in school systems and may check in on your son or daughter every week or once every two weeks. That is, if your child is in *special education*. Social workers also do therapy for parents, families and children. So, either one—psychologist or social worker—may greet you with *evaluations on your child*.

Evaluations are tricky things. Psychologists use tests, personal interviews with you and your child, and may also consult previous school, court or other records in forming decisions. Each decision carries with it a *diagnosis* of some sort. Social workers perform evaluations the same way except for tests; they are not eligible under law to administer tests.

So, here you are handed with an evaluation. What does it say? It says your child has a certain I.Q. or academic level, and it may detail problems reported by teachers or other staff. Evaluations also offer recommendations. Your child might qualify for certain educational or remedial services. Your child needs therapy. Or, your child is perfectly fine—it's you who needs the therapy. One way or another professional advice is offered. Unlike advice from a physician, this advice comes from *external, social or behavioral reasons.* Information deals with how the world affects your child from outside to inside, not the other way around. Aspects of behavior, emotion, thinking, and motivation are put through the ringer. You get the feeling from the evaluation that the psychologist knows your child better than you do.

But that's not true at all. Remember, you're the parent. You know your child better than anybody else does. Which brings up a problem. Evaluations can confuse you with the mumbo jumbo words and technical explanations. You can lose your socks if you personalize every word or take literally every result indicated. Don't do that. Instead, read over the evaluation like you were reading a magazine. Understand what you can and ask questions about the rest of it. Evaluations only tell what psychologists or social workers found *during testing and interviews. Evaluations do not reflect medical health, or direct observations of your child with people in the outside world.* Where "naturalistic" observations do occur, the evaluation may say more for you. Take from it what you need and can use for your own opinion. That's all you need to do.

Court System

Nothing is more frustrating than returning home after a long week of work or running errands, and opening a letter sent from the juvenile court system that says, "Ms. Smith, please be advised your son must appear before Honorable Judge Jacobs on Tuesday, March 15, for the alleged crimes of...." It just dribbles on and on and on. You knew it was coming, hired an attorney for it, and already saw your vacation money spent on legal and court fees. All for what? For your child's misbehavior getting so out of control that now it came to the attention of yet another expert. The juvenile court system. The process of adjudication is unpleasant for everybody, but especially for loving parents who must suffer the humiliation and disbelief of seeing a child treated like a common criminal. Even if your child really didn't commit a crime.

Entering this system happens for a number of reasons. First, your child did something illegal, from property destruction to breaking and entering to disorderly conduct, to bodily harm. And many variations in between. For this to happen, somebody pressed charges against your child and wants to see him get a court hearing. Other reasons your child may encounter the court system are to get away from you (emancipation) or as part of custody or placement (foster, adoption) purposes.

On a first offense the judge looks favorably upon your child's *other good habits* and may sentence your child to community service and a penalty fee ($200 to $500). But it all depends on what your child did wrong. An adolescent caught stealing at a department store got off easy. She had to devote 20 hours of voluntary time to a theater group within a month, and pay $200. She also remained on one-year probation requiring a monthly visit with her probation officer. Because she was in therapy at the time, no other demands were made. But stealing is one thing. Accessory to murder or breaking and entering is another thing. Those children are held, possibly without bond, in juvenile detention. That is a prison–like building of unhappy, young, adolescent men and women kept segregated except on occasion. They wait there until their court trials, until they are placed or until *they go somewhere else.*

But wherever they go and whatever happens to them, the one who really feels the pain is *you*. Hurt doesn't describe the half of it. Parents who witness their children incarcerated get the message loud and clear that they are bad parents and have no business raising children. Hate is felt all over the place. From the victims of crime to the judge, to the prosecuting attorney, to every single member of the jury or spectators in the courtroom. Nobody is sympathetic.

And so it becomes very difficult picking yourself up after being trampled on. You do it all right, just barely. But enough so that you can ask yourself, "is what they said about my son or daughter the gospel truth?" The answer is no, it's not. Court judgments and particularly opinions of judges are interpretations of law set down in writing from the many cases previous to what your child had. Sometimes the law describes a case that fits your child's case like a glove. Details differ, but judgment is influenced by the outcome of that case. Other times, matching a case is more difficult and there is no clear precedent. This is where the judge's decision humbly combines law and emotion. And, like the principal, that judge's opinion rests with evidence supplied from many sources. In this case, attorneys, witnesses, and your own child. Never consider that opinion the whole truth and nothing but the truth about your child's personality.

Okay, Let's Get Down to Basics

Everybody has an opinion. You can't get rid of them and you certainly can't change them, especially if through the court system. But you do have one way of getting back at all of them. Through a fine–tuned analysis of what's going on so that you can *really* know if your child has problems and what to do about it. The way to do this is by asking yourself many questions that cover all aspects of your child's misbehavior. You're trying to break down the problem into little pieces, searching each piece under a microscope until it is crystal clear. The following survey guides you in this direction:

Survey of Behavior Problem
1. Main problem
    a. Does your child have a behavior deficit?
    b. Does your child have a behavior excess?
    c. Does your child show avoidant behavior?

     d.   What does your child do well?

2.   **Clarify problem**

     a.   Who views the problem as objectionable?

     b.   What are the outcomes of the problem for the child and people around him or her?

     c.   What would be the outcomes be for the child and others if the problem was eliminated?

     d.   What happens right before the problem behavior?

     e.   Would the child have new problems if the problem was removed?

     f.   Is the child able to help in a solution to the problem?

     g.   What would the child or others gain if the problem was eliminated?

3.   **Clarify consequences**

     a.   What kind of rewards are most effective for this child?

     b.   What has been the experience with these rewards?

     c.   What adult or peer groups exert the most control over this child?

     d.   Does the child understand use of

rewards or punishers?

e. What are the child's unpleasant consequences (punishers)?

f. Would treatment require the child to give up current rewards associated with the problem behavior?

4. **Clarify any limitations**

a. Does the child have biological limitations that affect this problem?

b. Would these limitations (disabilities) restrict choice of treatment?

c. Is the problem behavior more pronounced when the child is hungry, thirsty or otherwise deprived of something?

5. **Clarify social changes**

a. Describe the child's present social and cultural situation (rural–urban, economic, ethnic/racial group, education, living quarters).

b. Can these situations be changed to assist with behavior change?

c. Before the current behavior problem, did the child exhibit similar behavior problems?

d. Can the current behavior problem be

traced to significant people or "Models" in the child's natural environment (home life, friends, school, etc.)?

6. **Clarify if there is self–control**

   a. Are there any situations in which the child can control the problem behavior?

   b. What are those situations and how does the child control the behavior?

   c. Does the child's perception of this problem correspond to observations by others?

   d. Can the child's ability to use self–control be used in treatment?

7. **Clarify interpersonal relationships**

   a. Who are the significant people in the child's life?

   b. Do certain people by mistake reward this behavior?

   c. What rewards are there in the child's social relationships?

   d. Can these people positively influence the child toward behavior change?

8. **Clarify the setting for behavior problems**

   a. How does the child's behavior compare to the norms for this behavior by his or her peers?

b. Are the norms for this behavior the same in various places (school, home, in public, etc.)?

c. Are there in the child's world limitations that prevent rewards for good behavior?

d. Does the child's natural environment permit the type of changes felt needed?

Now take a breath of air. You finished answering all these questions. What they in effect guide you toward is knowing if your child really is bad because people say she is bad, or is bad because situations around your child make her bad. If teachers and principal say your child is bad, but all kids are bad in that class, how *really bad is she?* If psychologists and social workers say your child is bad, and around you he is wonderful, does that mean your child really is bad? You need to know. The more facts made known to you, the more you know who to believe about your child's condition.

When Is Bad Behavior Really Okay?

A myth exists that negative feedback from everybody and his brother usually means there really is a problem. They can't *all* be lying, can they? Somebody must be telling the truth about your child's horrible behavior. Principal, teacher, doctor, psychologist—it has to be somebody. But who?

Maybe, just maybe they are all a little bit right, and a little bit wrong. Flaws in advice are common because the experts lack critical data on many different sides of your child, from social to biological, to psychological. Everybody doesn't know everything. So, if pieces of the puzzle are scrambled together in confusion, could it be possible the bad behavior is not always bad? Are there some occasions where *bad behavior is actually acceptable behavior?* Hard to believe, but true. Here are the ways your child's misbehavior may not be as bad as many people think:

When It's the Norm

Awful behavior is only awful if your child stands out in a crowd. Once all members of the crowd do that awful behavior, your child no longer stands out like a sore thumb. This is true for any closed or "contained" situation where there are groups of children together for long periods of time, like a classroom. A loud, rowdy, unsupervised classroom filled with 5th graders shouting obscenities and running around like it's a playground is the perfect setting. Here every child contributes equally to misbehavior and no one child can be singled out as the provoker.

That means, the ones who do stick out are the quiet, well–behaved ones, whereas *the norm of the classroom is to be disruptive.* When the average student is a noisy student, then noisiness may not be right and it may not be acceptable. *But,. at least it's not deviant. Not in that particular environment as long as those norms exist.* Make sure your child does not take the blame or become the scapegoat for a noisy classroom.

When It's Part of Child Development

Physicians and psychologists may catch on to this problem. The problem is your child is acting out because that is what most children do around this age group. That doesn't mean children automatically do this misbehavior, but that it is common and should not be treated as mental illness. Examples are 2 to 3 year olds having temper tantrums. Cliches about the "terrible twos" help keep this in perspective. Even talking back to parents by age 8, 9 and particularly into adolescence is relatively normal. So is petty theft in the child's early teens. That doesn't mean these behaviors are pleasant, or even acceptable; but all children undergo behavior and personality changes bearing similar patterns, no matter how much of an individual they are.

When It's Part of Being Physically Ill

Medically ill children suffering from asthma, cancer, obesity, or physical disabilities have a disadvantage on the evaluation scene. They are prone to misdiagnosis. Experts may forget that illness limits physical stamina, limits attention span, that pain produces aggression, and that few social skills develop. Disabled kids have many skill deficits from lacking the many opportunities to be part of the regular world. They also have excesses. Behaviors may get out of control because the few people they *do deal with give too much attention to their bad behaviors.*

Consider a state school for the blind. These are facilities operated in every state for blind school children who have multiple disabilities and cannot function in regular special education classes in public school. Students on the campus attend classes like public school students, but they also do something very different. At night they sleep in dormitories like students do on a college campus. Imagine this, now. Eight, nine, ten year olds, even 14 year olds living among their peer group in a residential dormitory 5 days a week, eating and sleeping together. It's tough enough imaging healthy (nondisabled) eight, nine, ten year olds, even 14 year olds pulling this off—for just 1 or 2 months. Ask any summer camp counselor, he or she will tell you the mayhem. But no, we're talking everyday for 10 months out of the year—and these children are not even physically healthy.

The moral of the story is this: *if healthy kids who know how to socialize can't pull it off without problems, how in the world are disabled kids who don't know how to socialize going to do it?* That is why state schools for the blind and schools for the deaf show records of enormous behavior problems in all aged children.

When It Happens in Spurts, not Everyday

Ever hear of the saying, "one swallow doesn't make a summer?" No? That's okay, few people have. The saying means that if something happens once, don't necessarily expect it to happen again or mean anything in particular. Behavior disruptions are like that. One day your calm, huggable child cozies with you by the fire in the family room. Pajamas on, afghan snuggling the two of you together. The next morning you feel like you went back in time to Shakespeare's *Merchant of Venice*. Your so–called loveable child is yelling, screaming, calling you names and it feels like your heart has been gutted. The reason? It's simple. Your child is entitled to a bad day.

Many reasons explain the once–in–awhile or *episodic* outbursts children have at home or in school. Sickness, fatigue, hunger, thirst, bathroom needs—are some among many reasons. Or, bursts of anger happen when your child loses a special toy, or is upset when it doesn't do what he or she wants it to do. Case in point is playing with Legos. Those little delicate pieces snap together in sequence if and only if your child has the coordination of a spider— and most children don't. Most children get frustrated if red pieces fall off yellow pieces, and stand–up little people fall down. Legos were built for children with emotional and physical stamina. Yet even the young aspiring architects of tomorrow lack this stamina at their tender age. Does it mean they never will enjoy Legos? Of course not. But once in a while, or episodically, frustration erupts uncontrollably. It's not a crisis. Not even a mini-crisis.

When It's Side–Effects of Medicine

Behavior problems also arise from side-effects of medicine. A recovering child still on antihistamines or other cold medicines may be groggy, inattentive to details and irritable. Think about what you feel like under medication and trying to fight off a miserable cold. Your child feels twice as bad because his petite body and weaker immunity system are working double time.

Medicine prescribed for other ailments or pain can also cause weird side–effects. A young male adult (age 17) receiving a mild dose of Percodan for a tooth ache, even after oral surgery on it, may feel very mellow, slow, and lethargic. After the Percodan wears off, sensations change quite a bit. Now your child feels like a live wire; very tense, eery, nervous energy, no appetite and wide awake. Withdrawal symptoms may last for a night or into morning, as your child says and does things way out of whack for his personality. He chatters nonstop about anything and everything; he paces the floors back and forth; he starts one activity but changes it to another activity; he is short–tempered. All in all, his temperament is very excitable. And why? Because the medicine is creating strange withdrawal sensations that cause him to do bad behavior.

When To Seek Therapy

Even when bad behavior really is "okay," how long will it stay "okay?" A short time? Perhaps a month or two, maybe longer? Bad behavior started by mistake from physical illness or medication side–effects can even turn sour if it becomes out of control. One parent, for example, told of his 2 year old son suffering from asthma and congenital heart failure. He and his wife watched him like a hawk, day and night, nursing his needs. When he cried, "we were right there seeing what was wrong. Anything Brad wanted he got. Maybe we were too protective of him, but we thought it would nurse him back to health."

But Brad's "I want everything right now" behavior became impulsive. A medically ailing child got so much attention that he now expects that attention all the time. Even when he is not ill—that's when there is a problem.

There are other examples of so–called "okay" behavior getting out of hand. Bridget played a joke on her 3 year old sister Sarah using fake vomit. Every time her sister walked into the kitchen, she teased her in front of their mother for vomiting. And Sarah laughed at first. But the joke got stale after the tenth time. Then Sarah was afraid of the vomit. When Sarah *felt ill and really needed to vomit, she couldn't do it. It was too scary.*

And how about the case of two brothers. Brothers always pick on each other, don't they? Daniel thought so. He was 15 and his younger brother, Bruce, was 8. Daniel got a big kick out of punching his brother for the fun of it. At first the two brothers "pretended to punch" each other while they wrestled on the floor. Daniel on top of Bruce, locking his head into place and teasing to slug him. Then Daniel really did slug him...just for laughs. And both of them laughed. For Daniel the joke kept going. He jabbed Bruce in the ribs and on the shoulder every time he passed him in the hallway at home.

Was this so horrible? Won't *boys be boys?* No. Not in this case. Bruce become so accustomed to being hit that he felt this *must be how people who are cool interact. So, now Bruce started hitting kids at school, hitting his younger sister, Sheila, and teasing his brother Daniel so Daniel would hit him again. By accident, playfulness transformed into dangerous bad behaviors that now interfere with daily life.* That's the first reason why you should consider seeking therapy. That is, *really* seeking therapy. Here are the other reasons.

GO TO THERAPY:

1. When child or parent actions interfere with daily life.
2. When everybody sees the problem except you.
3. When you're out of solutions.
4. When you want to learn something.
5. When you and your child can gain skills
6. When your child has other behavior or emotional

When Child or Parent Actions Interfere with Daily Life

What does that mean "behavior interferes with daily life?" It means your child's bad actions are so *frequent, severe, and disruptive upon others without control.* Behavior of all types gets out of control, even after trying *everything you can to stop it from happening*. You feel defeated, battle fatigued, and annoyed at your child's actions—that's also a warning sign of "out of control." Bad behavior also disrupts your normal day or prevents you from doing things you must do.

An executive administrator for a state office could not get her work done. Excuse after excuse, she would leave her office for an hour here, hour there, hoping her boss understood her reasons. "It's Jessica, again." Urgent calls from the daycare, from the school, from almost everywhere—all saying the same thing. "Come pick up your daughter because we can't handle her." Jessica's tantrums, yelling, screaming, running around, and horrible disrespect throws the staff into orbit. They don't know what to do and unload their frustrations on your shoulder.

But after time, your shoulder breaks. You're sick and tired of rushing to rescue people from emotional collapse. It's time to do something about Jessica's behavior. Interruptions jeopardize your:

1. daily work schedule
2. marital or social relationships
3. relationship with your other children
4. trust and happiness going places outside the home

5.   love and interest being around the bad
        behaving child.

When Everybody Sees the Problem Except You

And usually you're right in the thick of it.
Engulfed in the flame of the fire. You try to stand
back and seriously question if interruptions and
problems are really your child's fault. You put on
your thinking cap and look at it like a spectator. But
no matter how detached you try to become, your
perception is still too subjective. You see a
wholesome child, not a troublemaker.

That's why it pays, sometimes, to listen to
what other people say about your child's behavior.
As mentioned earlier, never take their opinions as
gospel. Nobody gets the full scoop, and there is
always some bias that sneaks in. Outsiders do,
however, have an advantage over you. They see
your child behave *and watch how you behave
toward your child*. That alone makes their input
worthwhile.

When comments from friends, relatives and
specialists all point a finger at your child's bad
behavior, there may be some truth to it. Don't
pooh, pooh it. Ask them exactly what behaviors
they believe are disruptive. Ask them also exactly

what they think you are doing or not doing when this bad behavior occurs.

When You're Out of Solutions

The warfare of managing child behavior need not be until *"death do us part."* Pushing to get your child under control at all costs, come "hell or high water," only frustrates the situation. It intensifies bad behavior and destroys what little patience you have left. Your determination to beat this behavior is admirable, but not necessary.

Many parents refuse to give up because defeat means you're incompetent or you're a failure. That "you failed at something so easy as controlling your child." You feel humiliated, inferior and blame your failure on all the ghastly, disrespectful actions your child does to ruin your parenting efforts. But there is no failure in running out of steam. It's nobody fault. So, stop blaming yourself. You exhaust your knowledge tank of good tries and advice people give you, but that's okay. You're entitled to run out of ideas, to literally not know what to do next. That's what therapy is for.

When You Want to Learn Something

Therapy adds to your knowledge of skills. Therapy is like school where you pick up ideas, strategies, insight, and the practical, how–to–use tools that are at your disposal at the moment you return home. Therapy is your opportunity to *learn critical parenting skills that refine what you already know or teach you what you don't know. Specific hands–on tactics that overcome interruptions and establish control over a behavior problem.*

Therapies focusing on specific parenting skills are very different from traditional therapy. Traditional therapy for children is play therapy. Play therapy draws emotional troubles out of your child by having them explore and manipulate toys. This allow them to act out frustrations and be free of anger so your child will know how much he hurts and needs love. But traditional therapy does not teach you, the parent, direct and structured skills.

Skills that handle your child's misbehavior come from *behavior therapies.* Behavior therapies also talk about your child's frustration and your headaches and failures, but only briefly. The real focus is upon *what you need to do for your child to bring that bad behavior under control.* Therapy for your child also emphasizes *what to do differently.*

When You *And* Your Child Can Gain Skills

The hardest part of seeking therapy is saying, "I don't know something and it is hurting my relationship with my child." Realize this problem. Years go by so quickly and that squeaky kid with pig tails grows up into an adolescent right before your eyes. You build a healthy, strong and trusting relationship with her before and then you won't feel it's too late to be a parent. That's why starting early, when you first spot signs of behavior problems, is to your advantage. Make the confession even if it stings you or chokes you with guilt. Admit to yourself that, "yes," I need to learn real strategies that nobody ever taught me—and my child also needs help."

Funny, isn't it? Sometimes we seek help naturally. Suppose you went swimming with friends and saw them doing the breast stroke. But all you knew was the dog paddle. You might naturally think, "You know, I should take swimming lessons one day. Yeah, I've got to do that." Suppose you went dancing with your spouse. He waltzed around the floor like a swan—Fred Astaire in person. And you—well, a perfect candidate for the "Two–Left Feet" award. You might naturally think, "You know, I should take dance lessons one day. Yeah, that's a good idea." So good of an idea that you sign up for one right away.

Signing up for therapy is the same thing. When you see weak skills in yourself, give therapy a call. Treat the idea of therapy just as you do swimming class or dance class—as just another class. A class on parenting skills or skills on eliminating self–guilt, anger, and personalizing what your child does. Therapy might not improve your swimming strokes or dance steps, but it goes a long way to restoring love for your kids.

When Your Child Has *Other* Behavior or Emotional
Problems

So far the problem behaviors discussed in this book vary from tantrums to noncompliance. We've also covered lying, stealing, anger, and being disrespectful. These behaviors make up the bulk of daily problems facing most parents or are seen at early stages of major behavior problems. But what about *other major behavior problems?*

Decisions to go to therapy depend on what your child is or is not doing, whether that behavior, good or bad, is extreme. Is it excessive? Is it deficient? Or has the behavior gone too far, beyond either extreme so that it enters the *danger zone?* A behavior in the danger zone takes five major forms. These behaviors require instant professional attention or else your child may get worse and worse, making the behavior harder to treat in adulthood.

BEHAVIORS IN THE DANGER ZONE:

1. Attention Deficit (Hyperactivity) Disorder
2. Conduct Disorders
3. Anxiety Disorders
4. Eating Disorders
5. Developmental Disorders (Autism, emotional impairment, learning disability, dyslexia,etc.)

Attention–deficit (hyperactivity) disorder. Children having this problem are typically restless, impulsive, distractible and overactive, with short attention span. They have difficulty concentrating on any one activity or any one task for very long. They may have a hard time staying seated for long. They don't listen well, and are "on the go" all the time. Some parents and teachers even describe these kids as "off the wall."

Serious and persistent difficulties all revolve around (a) attention span, (b) impulse control, and (c) hyperactivity. Tendencies develop in infancy and evolve rapidly into acute stages where the following characteristics are frequently evident, the child:

1.   Fidgets, squirms or seems restless
2.   Has difficulty remaining seated.
3.   Is easily distracted.
4.   Has difficulty awaiting turn
5.   Blurts out answers
6.   Has difficulty following instructions
7.   Has difficulty sustaining attention.
8.   Shifts from one uncompleted task to another.
9.   Has difficulty playing quietly.
10. Talks excessively.
11. Interrupts or intrudes on others.
12. Does not seem to listen.
13. Often loses things necessary for tasks.
14. Frequently engages in dangerous actions.

Conduct   disorder. Conduct disorder is antisocial behavior or delinquent behavior similar to that discussed in Chapter 5, about lying, stealing, being insensitive and drawing the attention of the criminal justice system. Conduct means "severely emotional behaviors" where your child is aggressive, argumentative, a bully, or physically or verbally dangerous to others. Fifteen year old Troy was like that. He snuck out of his bedroom every night without his parents knowing it. Then he met his 18 year old friends on the street and they made their way to an abandoned grocery store. They broke in, just for the fun of it. It was exciting. But it was getting late. So, they slept the night away in the back of a cargo train.

Behavior so deviant like this that it "breaks the code of normal child routines" and is extreme for typical bad behaviors, puts the child at risk. Troy never considered the "danger involved." It never occurred to him his parents may worry about him or that sneaking out of his bedroom is *wrong to do*. Actions are on impulse, *because the excitement of doing something is stronger than the fear of being bad*.

Anxiety disorder. Disturbed behaviors include anxiety and depression. Anxious children are always on edge, always afraid, always unhappy and ready for catastrophes. They are perfectionists, obsessive–compulsive, even phobic. Preschoolers may cry a lot or seem fearfully shy. Adolescents hide in their bedrooms, keep a low profile, withdraw from friends or stay clear of the popularity contests.

Eating disorder. Children suffer cyclical weight gains and losses just like adults. But for children the need for thinness is at times obsessive. How important is it, for example, that middle school aged Jessica look slim and trim for her friends? *Very important*. Jessica may want to look popular, may want "guys" to look at her, may want to be a cheerleader or just to look all–around attractive so everybody thinks she is fabulous. *Behaving fabulous is not enough. You also have to look fabulous to get the prize.* And so every adolescent and early adult child goes through strenuous auditions for being the perfect physical specie. *At any cost*.

The price of perfection is at the root of eating disorders. Warning signals trigger when eating or not eating is no longer a habit, but becomes a preoccupation. Worried about getting fat, kids may starve themselves or go on strict diets. Deliberately not eating or eating in small bites leads to *anorexia nervosa*. A disorder marked by constant loss of body weight through starvation. But starving is not for everybody. Some kids love food too much to abandon it altogether. So, there is another trick to the trade. Diet when you can and *shame on you if you eat too much. Because you must get rid of that surplus fat before you realize you're fat.*

Removal of "fat" is done the wrong way. Kids take laxatives or induce themselves to vomit. They think this eliminates excess rapidly and restores their bodies to a pre–fat state. But the habit that develops from this action is *bulimia nervosa.* A habit characterized by upward and downward swings in weight, and the exhausting fear of feeling too full.

Younger children slip into other types of eating disorders not popular among the adolescent crowd. A child who is impulsive and gets away with sneaking food whenever desired can become obese. *Obesity* is not a crime, but it is embarrassing for children. Heavy weight also expands cellular structure at an early age that makes weight gain a constant problem as your child gets older and especially in adulthood. "Fat kids" get teased, pushed around, and are made scapegoats for their unusual size. When feeling like a fool, large kids resign to being a fool. It hurts their self–esteem, academic grades and motivation for friends.

At younger ages, eating take another bizarre form. Two year old Lora had a great appetite. Give her fruit and she'd gobble it up in seconds. Offer her candy, and down the pipe it went. Just like the wallpaper. She could make a feast out of it. Wallpaper, an inedible substance, developed a stimulating interest for her like food because *she chewed it, swallowed it and* digested it just like food. But it wasn't really food. Nonfood substances that children eat are a condition called *pica*.

And, to some extent, most children experiment with the world of inedibles. After a while, yucky taste and reprimands from parents fade out the exploratory interests, and food preferences return to normal. A pica child is different. He or she persists with this intrigue despite parental warnings. And the danger, of course, is that uncontrolled taste samples of nonfoods may harm your child if the substance is painful, poisonous, or lethal.

Developmental disorder. A "developmental" disorder means something went wrong in the learning stages of growth. Interruptions in healthy learning come from all sources. A child struck with too much punishment may hide in a shell of fear. Excessive fears may turn a child inward, where she does not respond to people or refuses to develop language at all. This is an *autistic child*. Autism has these features:

1.   Your child is not attentive to people. He acts aloof, avoids eye contact, won't cuddle or tolerate physical contact, and doesn't play with other children.

2.   Your child has severe language impairment. He is mute, or may just repeat what you say or say it backwards or repeat a statement many times.

3.   Your child is strongly resistant to change. He has tantrums when normal routines are altered. He has many rituals or rigid patterns of activity.

4.   Your child rarely has opportunities for appropriate play with toys.

5.   Your child has hyper– (too much) or hypo– (too little) sensitivity to sight, taste, smell, touch and hearing.

6.   Your child does a lot of self–stimulation. He rocks back and forth, waves his hands around, spins

objects, twirls himself around or does other rhythmic, repetitive motions.

7.   Your child gets "really" hard to manage. He cries and tantrums go berserk. He bites himself, knocks his head against the wall, tears his skin, hits other people randomly or is viscously destructive.

8.   Your child has an obsessive fascination with objects. More than hugging a teddy bear. He talks to it *or talks for it, all the time.*

Other developmental disorders seen frequently in preschool and school age children are *learning disabilities and emotional impairment*. A learning disability (LD) is a deficiency in some basic academic or functional skill (reading, writing, math, language, etc.) limiting your child from performing like his peers. Disabilities in reading and writing (Dyslexia), for example, consist of slow or fragmented efforts. Your child may write his name backwards, or a letter backwards, may struggle to hear syllables, vowels or have a tough time connecting meanings.

Emotional impairments strictly deal with behaviors that interfere with learning.

Hyperactivity is an emotional impairment. So is inattention to details or daydreaming. Disturbing classmates not once, or twice but in place of *doing anything productive all day,* is another example. Children who are impulsive, aggressive, or at the extreme opposite are bashful and timid, never do good on tests and bomb on homework. They may know *how to do the assignment and may even find school work easy, but frustrations or fears contaminate their ability to concentrate.*

Watch Out for Labeling Your Child

So, at least, that's what the school psychologists tells you. And the social worker supports it. Teachers' agree with this conclusion, and the principal stands behind his staff. Virtually anyone dealing with your son or daughter now is convinced they have a disability or emotional impairment. The hard part is: Can they convince you of this?

The proof still is in the pudding. You ask for test results, for evaluation results. You ask how your *disabled or impaired* child compares to other children their age. You ask for a second opinion. Then you take your child to the physician. He agrees with the school. Then to a psychologist for a third opinion. He also agrees with the school. Still not satisfied, you shuttle your child around town from specialist to specialist hoping for differences of opinion. But it doesn't happen. Each specialists evaluating your child agrees there is a problem. "Yes, your child has a disability or is impaired."

It still doesn't feel right. You want to know why? It feels funny just *labeling your child.* Being called "fatty," "four–eyes," even racial and ethnic slurs are bad enough. Tolerating these attacks through life takes guts and lots of stamina to ignore them. But at least verbal assaults like "string–bean" and "tuna–breath" are partly a tease and partly kids' play. Nobody is really a "string–bean." Few kids, even those upset at being called names, talk themselves into thinking they are actual string-beans.

But not so with labels. Negative labels are not kids' play. Once you hear your child is *emotionally impaired or has a learning disability,* you might as well have heard he had rabies. The feeling of pain is the same. Labeling leaves a bad taste in you mouth because you begin to associate your child with the thing he is called. From your child has "emotional impairment," comes *he is emotionally impaired.* From your child has "learning disabilities" comes *he is learning disabled*. Labels no longer describe aspects of your child. Now they are the parts of which he is made.

Effects of labeling upon parents is half the problem. The other half is how kids' react to them. First is your kids. Second is your kids' friends.

Your kids. Your child is like an abandoned raft drifting back and forth in open water trying to set a course. Nowhere to go except where adults tell him to go. Labeled children may have no idea exactly what their label means or why they got the label but they do know one thing: *nobody else has that label.* And for some strange reason, those having that label are *treated differently—not better, but worse.* Confused, your child grasps for meaning on what is going on and the answers he gets all too often are very mean and painful.

Children labeled emotionally impaired and learning disabled get treated like lepers. There's no question about it. Efforts in the last 20 years for "special education" classrooms have been better, so that exceptional children receive equal opportunities for education. That's the good part. And, all in all, this plan of equal education tries vigorously to be fair, supportive, and enriching. But there's a part of special education that lawmakers never bargained for when Public Law 94–142 passed in 1975. That healthy, nonspecial education children would regard those "other kids" as rejects, weirdos, and retards.

Locally, for example, there is a special school and closed sheltered workshop for retarded individuals called "Beekman Center." It is a fine school and provides superior training with hard–working staff. But in the public schools nearby or even within a 20 mile radius, any kid who acts dumb or is in special education (emotionally impaired or learning disabled) is called "A BEEKMAN." By reference, special education kids never have a chance. They are automatically earmarked as strange, alien, and off their rocker no matter how friendly or sweet that child is. He or she is A BEEKMAN.

The trouble with labeling is that children react to the *label and not the behavior that deserved the label*. Parents do this also. So do professionals. This leads to four major problems with labeling a child:

The Problem with labeling a Child is that—

1. *The child begins to perceive himself as that label and loses self–esteem, sense of accomplishment, and motivation.*

2. *People dealing with that child use circular reasoning to explain why the child has a problem.* Such as this off–the–wall thinking: "Why did Billy yell at his teacher yesterday? Oh, yes, it's because he's emotionally impaired. That explains it. That's what emotionally impaired kids do."

3. *It distracts parents, professionals and kids away from what your child really is doing.* From his behavior. All that is looked at is the label. Good behavior, bad behavior, even fluctuations between both, all reflect *what kids with that label typically do.* No credence is given to the behavior itself. A parent recently said to me that her daughter's poor concentration and tantrums were *because she had an attention–deficit disorder.* That automatically explained it. Forget any other reasons for the behavior itself.

4. *Treatment only cures the label, not the behavior.* This is a serious problem. Experts, teachers, and parents forget that labels only describe

what a child is doing, not what a child has turned in to. A yelling and screaming child who is "off the wall" is not a hyperactive child. Instead, *his behavior is hyperactive.* If you think this is a game of words, you're mistaken. Imagine people saying you're an awful tasting person after you bombed on some chocolate chip cookies. It sounds weird, right? *You're not awful tasting, the cookies are awful tasting. The cookies are something you did. So, something you did is awful tasting. The way to correct that awful taste is to correct how you make cookies.*

That's simple enough. But look what happens in translation to labels. Your child is yelling, screaming and tantruming. Does correcting this behavior mean correcting the hyperactivity ("bad–tasting person") or *the behaviors that cause the hyperactivity* ("how you baked the cookies)? Obvious as this answer is "yes, correct the behavior," most parents, experts and teachers do not see it this way. Frequently medicines are prescribed to children for control of hyperactivity (attention–deficit disorder), and for control of other emotional impairments. Medicines that calm anxiety or slow down the pace. On medicines like Ritalin, Cylert, or Dexedrine, hyperactive children supposedly function normally and for longer periods of time.

But Ritalin and other stimulant or depressant drugs have become highly controversial. There are many persons who oppose the use of these drugs in children completely. They say that hyperactivity can be a symptom of a number of physical disorders such as cardiac problems, low blood sugar, calcium deficiency, and petit mal seizures. Conditions which need other types of treatment. The opponents also argue that elementary schools usually stifle children, requiring them to sit still and be quiet all day long. And that hyperactive children are often healthy children who are rebelling against a system which does not allow them to express themselves freely. To the opponents, Ritalin in these children is *drugging them into submission.*

There is no doubt that Ritalin and other medicines have been abused as the opponents charge. Different school systems have varying policies with regard to medicine. There are schools in which a teacher can request that a child be considered for Ritalin and where the school can order parents to give that drug to their child even if they do not wish to do so.

However, opposite school policies can be found as well. Some schools consider Ritalin a last option. Instead, psychologists and consultants look at whether a child's weak performance irritates his teacher or leads to harassment at school. The organic causes of behavior may be minor compared to the profound social punishment a child gets for *behaving unlike his peers*. So, as long as parents, teachers, and specialists look at the big picture of behavior problems first, more will be known about *why your child does what he does*, and the choice of medicine may be one among many options.

Finding a Therapist

People are still afraid of the stigma of seeing a therapist. Consequently, names and types of therapists are not readily available or familiar to most people. But to the emotionally troubled parent, finding the right therapist can be a traumatic experience. With numerous psychiatrists, psychologists, social workers, and paraprofessionals around, plus countless types of therapies—people stumble into a paradox of endless questions and few answers. It is mind–boggling trying to keep up with the fast–paced revolution of therapies and psychologic gurus around the country. Nevertheless, the frightened onlooker enchained by his or her own uncertainties is determined for a better lifestyle, but doesn't know which way to turn.

Realizing there are thousands of therapists and therapies is a beginning. The next step is shopping around for therapies. Shoppers are said to be bargain hunters. Systematic or not, these undertakings are a positive sign of consumerism. Of course there is the easy way out. Nonshoppers go for nonprofessional helpers. There is increasing recognition that neighbors, hairdressers, work supervisors, bartenders, and cab drivers, naming only a few, are good listeners, armchair psychologists with an open ear and fist full of advice. Nonprofessional helpers are less costly and of course relieve the person from admitting they need professional attention.

But as views of therapy pivot from being a "stigma" to the "in-thing," it becomes less embarrassing saying that you and your child are in therapy. Eliminated are the myths that therapy is for lunatics and failures. You're not a lunatic, neither is your child. You're perfectly healthy people making the best out of life and realizing there are concrete obstacles in the way of that path.

That's why you seek therapy: Not to confess your sins, but to reap specific benefits on putting your life back on course.

Shopping for Effective Therapy

So you are ready to find a therapist. That's good. That's the first step. Wonderful! But there is one slight problem. *How do you do it?* Choosing a specialists is a sticky issue involving many important questions along the lines of:

1. Do you want somebody for yourself or your child?
2. Do you want somebody specializing in children and families?
3. Do you want somebody focused on teaching you, not analyzing you?
4. Do you want somebody at a reasonable cost?
5. Do you want somebody who holds sessions (45 to 50 minutes per session) in the evenings, on weekends?
6. Do you want a male or female therapist?
7. Do you want a person with a good track record? If so, how do you get that track record?
8. Where do I get leads on therapists?

And these are only some of the questions. Many more pop up when considering that *this person will be someone you talk to personally and who knows more about you than most people in your life*. That takes some thinking about. So, let's think about it.

Somebody for Yourself or Your Child? Who needs therapy the most? Your child? You? Maybe your spouse? All three candidates probably earn the Oscar nomination. But the difficulty is locating a therapist versatile enough to handle all three people or willing to handle therapy that way. Needs for yourself require a therapist who works with adults, *primarily* or with families. That therapist should be familiar with key issues facing today's parents, from two–family incomes to division of labor in the household. Most practitioners are not this ambidextrous. Either they specialize in adults or in children, or with families. Best way is to ask the individuals what they specialize in.

Therapists who do work with adults and children may refuse to see you *and your child* for another reason. Conflict of interest. Tradition in therapy holds that loyalty to one client may interfere with loyalty to another client, no matter the age. Compare this to having one attorney represent yourself and your spouse during a hot divorce. Who really is in your corner? Many therapists build trust with one client and feel it may collapse if other family members also see that therapist. That is why the therapist seeing you may advise *seeking another therapist for your child.*

However, truth is that sharing therapists rarely if ever damages rapport, trust or process of therapy. Therapists in fact obtain insider facts that make the task of treatment *easier, faster, and more effective* since they already know the family history and can anticipate parental or child reactions under certain situations. Advantages of knowing what's going on far outweigh the burden of coordinating stories with another therapist, who may be reluctant to release confidential information even with your permission. The best bet, then, is obtaining a therapist who readily accepts seeing you and your child.

Should the two of you be seen together, or separately? Again, tradition plays a role here. The standard is split. Family therapies center on mom, dad, child, and his or her siblings all participating together in a team approach at solving the problem. Like any system, underlying this approach is that no one person can make changes better than a group of people. And there is wisdom to this approach. But team energies can still work if the therapist meets alone with each person .

Some therapists go about it this way. Depending on the age of your child, therapy may start with the parents who learn methods of behavior control. Sessions also occur once or twice with your child focused on anger control or some direct teaching. Once you feel there is progress on your behalf, and evidence of improvement in your child, sessions start with you and your child. These sessions are for practicing skills you learned in your session and your child in his sessions. Skills are fine tuned under the watchful eye of therapist and practice assignments now involve a team. By comparison, this approach to therapy offers individual plus parent–child structure producing the best results.

Somebody specializing in Children? This is a must. Family therapists are a good beginning and especially if your child's problem is secondary to other major problems, such as horrible marital fights, or one partner abuses drugs and alcohol, having an affair or causing another family disturbance. Where maritally things are stable, find out if the family therapist is competent in pediatric psychology. Any therapist can claim this expertise. One or two classes and a good book on child growth and counselors may feel they earned their stripes. But that's not enough. Pediatric psychologists spend their whole practice or a big part of it knowing how children act, react, and can be expected to function under all sorts of situations. Trust specialists who are clearly credentialed, licensed or who can prove speciality with kids.

The other advantage of having a "Kiddie Shrink" is so your child can feel at home. Strange as you might feel in the counselor's office, your child really feels out of place. For them this person is a stranger, and the place unfamiliar to them. Even familiar toys or playing with their own toys just doesn't re-create the "home-sweet-home" atmosphere. Child specialists know this and are immediately ready to make your child trust them. Decorations, candy containers, and open arms greet your child the first time she lays eyes on this alien nation.

Somebody focused on teaching you, not analyzing you? "For goodness sake, Dr. Freud, isn't there anything I can do about this situation?" How much should a therapist get to know you—really know you—before giving you advice? Should you receive advice at all, or just come to it on your own?

Here's the bottom line: Feelings of helplessness walking out of a therapist's office is a bad sign. You came to this person for the same purpose that you go to your physician. To get answers. You want answers on how to cure a problem causing you grief. At the physician's office you seek cures or solutions for physical grief. Your physician examines you, describes possible reasons for the symptoms, and prescribes a course of treatment. Well, therapists *should be expected to provide the same approach.* You explain your difficulty or that of your child's, the therapist assesses important facts, including details about family history, and *should then prescribe a series of systematic steps toward eliminating the problem.*

Many therapists protest this rapid process, saying they hate to make hasty conclusions until all the facts are in. But how long does it take to accumulate facts? One session, two sessions, maybe a month worth of sessions? Too many sessions are wasting your time. Specialists who really know children, parents and families can size up situations after the first 15 minutes let alone the first session.

Not because they are "crystal–balling" the diagnosis, that is, guessing the best they can using stereotypes, myths, and assumptions. The reason is that therapists know families demonstrate *patterns*. Patterns reflect how family members interact, why they interact, and outcomes of these interactions. For every pattern there are predictable behaviors, consequences, and chain reactions affecting the entire family unit. These can be detected in the first meeting.

So, it is not necessary to spend hours upon hours or many sessions analyzing yourself, your child, or your family under the banner of "we'll get to a solution sooner or later, just be patient." No, don't be patient. Get annoyed and ask that therapist to offer practical strategy on what to do about problem behaviors.

That leads to what "teaching you" is all about. Therapists who teach are showing in every session the next step or repeating steps in a series of child management skills. Warmth, friendship, and caring still are offered to you, but toward a very solid goal. In the first session the therapist should share his or her impressions on the behavior problem, perhaps even suggest types of methods needed for behavior improvement. By the second session your therapist should outline a specific plan of attack. Identified are the exact goals of therapy and how the two of you propose to accomplish them. Each session after that introduces new or reviews old strategies, troubleshoots roadblocks, and encourages your perseverance to make strategies work. Anything less than this structured approach and you're wasting your money.

Somebody at a reasonable cost? Let's face it. Therapy is not cheap. Some things in life are. But therapy is not one of them. Price shopping is still a good idea because just as therapists differ in style, so do their fees. Today's skyrocketing costs for psychiatrists (M.D.s, D.O.s) may be out of your price range unless you have *insurance.* Costs per hour vary from $95 to $120 for single sessions. And if multiple sessions a week are necessary, at least for a month or so, the price figure climbs to a mighty peak. Down the slope a bit are psychologists (Ph.D.s) who currently charge between $50 to $90 per hour. And still farther downward are Masters–level counselors or social workers at $25 to $60 per hour.

"So costly?" Yes it is. Except there's a catch. Most practitioners accept third–party insurance or participate in some type of insurance plan. And with health insurance programs growing in epidemic proportions, it's a wise idea to know exactly where your mental health benefits stand. That is, *if you have mental health benefits*. But most people do. Third–party insurance usually takes one of these forms:

1.   *PPO*
2.   *HMO*
3.   *Copayment, direct reimbursement*
4.   *No copayment, direct reimbursement*

Traditional health insurance plans like Blue Cross and Blue Shield, Aetna, Travelers, among others, are beating the pavement to keep one step ahead of hungry PPOs and HMOs. A PPO is a preferred provider organization or coalition among physicians and other specialists to offer services at discounted rates as long as referrals stay within the circle of fraternity. Your child specialist, psychologist or social worker must either already participate in this PPO or be referred to by a PPO provider.

HMOs are even more strange. There are two dominant types of HMOs, which stand for Health Maintenance Organizations. First type is when all medical, psychological, dental and even visual services are in–house within one agency or organization. That means you go to the same building or group of counselors every time new problems pop up. HMOs also limit the number of therapy sessions. Philosophically, they hope fewer sessions encourages briefer therapy and motivation for rapid change. On average, total yearly allotments are about 20 sessions, with few exceptions. After 20 the client may have a copayment.

Another type of HMO is where you select your therapist outside the "agency." But that therapist must be a participating provider of the HMO, which means he or she agrees to lower rates and possibly even a withholding of 2% to 5% of reimbursement until the end of the fiscal year. This is so that watchdogs of HMO providers can have leverage in case a provider gets too sloppy or uses too many sessions.

Copayment and no copayment with direct reimbursement pertains to traditional health insurance. Here you find whoever you want as long as that therapist is a covered benefit. Some insurances, for example, promise great benefits but deliver peanuts. Other insurances stipulate that providers must meet certain minimum qualifications such as their degree, level of licensure, or types of therapy. Hypnosis, for instance, on curing your obsessive anger toward your daughter, may provide fantastic results for you. Miraculous changes in only a few weeks. But most insurance companies do not recognize and will not cover hypnosis. That means you get stuck with the large bill.

And that happens to a lot of people. A lick and a promise that your insurance will cover costs of therapy backfires when you receive the rejection of services notice—and panic. Now what? Now you do this: You do what millions of other people without insurance do to receive therapy. You contact your local community mental health agency. Federally and state funded agencies offer counseling and accept a *sliding fee schedule* for people on medicare, medicaid, or below the poverty level. Trained specialists are available at less or no cost at all. But the time you wait before starting therapy might be long. Waiting lists for community mental health counseling grow longer and longer each year, making it harder to use this cost–efficient alternative.

In the evening or weekend sessions? You know your schedule better than anyone. Daytime sessions may work out perfectly for you if you are by yourself, have only yourself to worry about, and distance between your home and the therapist is close. Sounds good, right? Dream on. Hardly the scenario for the average family in today's world. Your schedule never is so open or flexible that anytime of the day is fine for therapy. Just the opposite is true.

There is never a perfect slot open for therapy no matter how much shuffling around of activities you do. And further, who wants to take your child out of school each week? That's why you can ask for evening or weekend sessions. Many therapists working part–time or full–time recognize your busy schedule and will bend over backwards to accommodate your time requests within limits. After–work hours are common for therapists, some sessions even held at 9:00 pm or as early as 7:00 am. On the weekends, hours vary and it all depends on arrangements convenient for you and the therapist. *When* you meet is a very negotiable topic.

Male or female therapist? Will you get along with women better than men? Or, vice–versa? Intuitively, if you are a woman, you might expect another woman to be more sympathetic, insightful and on top of unique problems in your parenting experience. And especially if this female therapist has children—then she will *really know what I've been through,.* Men feel the same way about seeing male therapists. Oddly though, this gender–to–gender identity is a myth. For as many reasons, good and bad, you can think up for why you should see a female therapist, just as many reasons justify seeing a male therapist. The gender of therapist *is not as important in the short–run or long–run as much as how that therapist conducts the session.*

Meaning, is the therapist direct, expressive, and articulate about what needs to be done and how to do it? Does your therapist give you feedback, offer insight or redirect your thoughts toward positive, constructive ways of thinking and behaving? Is your therapist an active participant in the session? Answers of "yes" to these questions says a therapist is doing a valid job of treatment regardless of whether it is a he or she. Let your choice on male or female rest with the person's professional manner and behavior.

Somebody who has a good track record? How good is this therapist? Rumor has it that he or she cured a tantruming child in two months. Other rumors state it took one month. But what about for your needs? Does this hearsay information certify the therapist is perfect for you? A therapist with a good track record is one who meets client goals in effective, cost–efficient ways. You are usually familiar with some of the clients' success stories. Particularly the story from the person who referred you to that counselor. That friend of yours says about the therapist that he or she is:

1.   Consistent
2.   Caring
3.   Completes goals in about the same length for people with similar problems.
4.   Can support the strategies with case examples or hard data.
5.   Ethical and legal in therapy .

Ethics is the real delicate issue. Therapists who are up front about fees, about projected length of treatment, and about risks and benefits of treatment steps are upholding good ethics. They want your confidence in friendship and know that trust is the springboard to any lasting behavior changes in yourself or your child. Also, ethically–minded therapists are sensitive to your privacy, both in touch, and discussion. Questions regarding your sexual habits wait until the second, maybe third session. If personal probing must occur, the therapist might apologize up front for "embarrassing you" or "intruding on your life." Attention to these details not only shows genuine caring, but it builds your faith that positive things people have said about this therapist actually may be true.

Where do I get leads? From several places. Best leads come from family, friends, neighbors and trusted associates who freely disclose how this therapist helped them out of a jam. Such insider information creates a clear profile of expectations including any known faults the therapist has. Without second–hand knowledge, try these other resources:

1.   *Yellow Pages.* Professionals listed in the yellow pages are required by law to be licensed in some capacity. Listings may be under "family therapy," "mental health services," "marriage therapy," and "social workers," and "psychologists."

2.   *Newspaper advertisement.* Time was when professional ethics discouraged newspaper advertisement of clinical services. Rules changed and now clinics and single practitioners readily use paid ads for visibility. Check if the services listed in the ad, for example, on weight control or substance

abuse, follow proper credentialing, licensure or certification laws in your state. Many of these specialty programs require approval by state offices. For example, in Michigan, hanging a shingle out that says you treat substance abuse waves a red flag in front of the Department of Public Health. They must preview and license all agencies offering this service.

3.   *Mental health associations.* Local, state and nationwide groups frequently offer referral networks or have people on board willing to guide you to particular therapists. Associations never favor one therapist over the other but may recommend a *type of therapist appropriate for your needs*. Names of associations also can be found in the yellow pages.

4.   *Self–help and recovery groups.* The rising number of self–help and recovery groups in small and metropolitan areas offers a superb referral base for therapists. Groups like *Al–Anon, Alcoholics Anonymous, Divorce Support Group, Parents Anonymous, Overeaters Anonymous, Recovery, Adult Children of Alcoholics, Parents Without Partners, Tough Love, Survivors of Suicide, Stroke*

Support Group, among several more, consist of voluntary members assembled to share hurt, pain and explore solutions for growth. Members rely on the group for moral and emotional support but usually are in individual, family, or marital therapy as well. Once you feel comfortable at a meeting, ask a member or two for a therapist recommendation.

5. *Hospitals and community mental health centers.* Hospitals struck with reduced patient census, bitter cuts in staff, and desperate economic times find they can attract newcomers through specialty services. One such service is a referral network phoneline aimed at certain people, such as women or particular health impaired adults (stroke, Alzheimer's disease, diabetes, etc.). Calls to this service are free and you can receive referrals to physicians, psychologists or other providers usually associated with the hospital or a recognized expert in the field. Use the yellow pages under "hospitals" to find listed referral services.

6. *Your physician, dentist, attorney or specialist.* Probably the best referral resource are professionals you already trust, receive ongoing services from, and consider reliable friends. Ask your physician,

dentist, attorney (even hairdresser) for therapists they've heard about or worked directly with. Physicians keep a "private" list of therapists who handle medically–related emotional problems or follow into the category of *behavioral medicine*. Stress, hypersensitivity to body ailments, postoperative illness, and grief over cancer are examples. Your dentists surprisingly is an excellent resource for therapists handling eating disorders, particularly bulimia. Attorneys often work with therapists on evaluations of competency, child custody, substance abuse (drunk driving), and stress. They have endless good and bad news about providers in the community.

7.   *HMO, PPO or other health insurance.* Your own health insurance can provide referral information. Contact the agency or primary care physician (leader) assigned to you for advice. That office or person may recommend one person or may put you in touch with steps to follow in receiving mental health services. In some HMOs, for example, mental health services is a three–step process. First you telephone in about your need for therapy and receive an intake appointment. Intake appointments evaluate your situation, therapist

preferences, and whether therapy really is suitable for you at this time. Upon approval by a board or triage committee, you move on to the third step of being assigned a therapist.

When Does Therapy Work?

Sounds like an easy question, doesn't it? Won't you automatically know if therapy is improving you by how you feel or things you see different in your child? In one respect, yes, this is true. Casual observation of changes is a fine indicator that good things are happening. But improvements only signify you and your child are different, *not that these differences are due to therapy*. Because therapy should not work in strange and wondrous ways, you want to know if that $60 or $80 per session is really worth it. And you deserve to know.

Do You Like Your Therapist?

Start inspecting the effects of therapy after the second or third session. By then impressions are formed on liking or disliking your therapist and whether the stated goals really meet your target concerns. On liking your therapist, ask yourself several questions reflecting his or her manner and approach to problems. Questions like:

1. Do I feel comfortable with my therapist?
2. Is my therapist comfortable with me?
3. Is my therapist casual and informal rather than stiff and formal?
4. Does my therapist treat me as if I am sick, defective or about to fall apart?
5. Is my therapist flexible and open to new ideas rather than pursuing one point of view all the time?
6. Does my therapist have a good sense of humor and a pleasant disposition?
7. Is my therapist willing to tell me how he or she feels about me?
8. Does my therapist admit limitations and not pretend to know things he or she doesn't know?
9. Is my therapist willing to acknowledge being wrong and apologize for making errors or for being inconsiderate? Or does the therapist justify this kind of behavior?
10. Does my therapist answer direct questions rather than simply asking me what I think?
11. Does my therapist reveal things about

himself or herself either spontaneously or in response to my inquiries (but not by bragging and talking all the time).

12. Does my therapist encourage the feeling that I am as good as he or she is?

13. Does my therapist act as if he or she is my consultant rather than the manager of my life?

14. Does my therapist encourage differences on opinion rather than telling me that I am resisting if I disagree with him or her?

15. Is my therapist interested in seeing people who share my life? This would include family, friends, lovers, work associates, or any other significant people in my life?

16. Do the things my therapist says make sense?

17. In general, do my contacts with the therapist lead to my feeling more hopeful and having higher self–esteem?

Answers that show a theme of "yes, this person does help me, is open to my concerns, and treats me like an equal," are safe evaluations. Know your feelings about therapist and therapy early on before the need for therapy becomes too dependent or your own troubles scream out for *anybody* *no matter who they are.*

Knowing When Therapy Works

Good feelings about the therapist motivates you to try what he or she recommends, and stand behind advice given to your daughter or son. Your children may dislike therapists or regard their advice as crazy, totally irrelevant or just plain uncool. Kids who are disobedient or tantruming hardly take to another adult's opinions with open arms. But if you follow through on the therapist's methods, or on supporting your child's marginal efforts, progress can move along faster than you could ever imagine. So fast, that the need for therapy may last a short time.

How do you know when this time comes? What proof is there that weekly therapy is responsible for less and less tantrums, less and less family arguments, and surprisingly more affection between you and your children? Just what exactly is *the criteria to know when therapy works?* Consider the following six factors on whether therapy is helping you:

1.   Are there *measurable* changes in behavior?

2. Does behavior change improve self–esteem?

3. Does behavior change generate positive outcomes?

4. Does behavior change continue without relapse?

5. Is behavior change consistent with your purpose for therapy?

6. Does behavior change appear in many different places, not just at home?

Are there measurable changes in behavior? Ask yourself if progress is something you can visibly observe. Make it a numerical science. Before therapy your daughter never minded you. Today she minds you half the time—that's 50%. Or 50% more than she did before therapy started. Count the number of times she follows instructions, or number of times she doesn't follow instructions. Observed changes must be concrete and real. Good feelings about therapy or even toward your daughter don't count. You might discolor your honest opinion and may make improvement seem better than it actually is. But if you rely on hard data—on testing this good feeling with specific yardstick measurement, you'll be surprised at the superb results.

Does behavior change improve self–esteem? Learning to be calm and ride the tantrum until it fades is definitely progress. Control over your anger not only keeps you sane, but also eliminates wrong attention to your child for being bad. And that feels good. Really good. Suddenly you feel transformed from a stubborn, ornery parent to a cuddly soft–loving parent. All it took was putting certain methods into action in the right order, at the right times, and being consistent. Your son improves his behavior and *you feel much better about yourself for handling it so well.* Self–esteem leaps a hundred yards for every success story you have with your child.

Does behavior change generate positive outcomes? Your sense of serenity is half the goal. The other half is basking in the victory of having people around your son or daughter speak about how good your child behaves, or gives feedback to them directly. Positive remarks from friends, relatives, teachers, and even your spouse sparkle your child's personality and stimulate his desire to continue being loved. Positive outcomes shape appropriate behavior as well as provide new opportunities for even better behavior that were previously withheld. Now your child has access to rewards, treats and fun activities like the other children.

Does behavior change continue without relapse? Important to ask yourself is, "is this wonderful miracle of changes only a dream—or will I wake up in Kansas?" Doubt is a stubborn habit. You can't shake it so easily no matter how optimistic you are; the skeptic in you keeps it alive. And there's nothing wrong with doing this. Being skeptical about rapid progress does not mean you reject therapy or even discount the therapist's skills. It means *you are the one who lived with this problem child before therapy, during therapy, and will live with this child after therapy regardless of what happens.* So, before you raise a toast to victory, you just want double and triple protection against old behavior patterns slipping back .

That's what is meant by *relapse.*

Relapse happens for the following reasons.

1. YOU get lazy at using the prescribed steps for behavior control.
2. YOU forget about rewarding your child for prescribed behaviors.
3. YOU (AND YOUR SPOUSE) are inconsistent with the methods or rewards.

4.   **YOU** make concessions to your child, deviating from the plan. You might do this when visiting friends, grandparents, or other relatives. Also, exceptions might crop up at family or community activities.

5.   **YOU** revert back to old habits of handling bad behavior. Returning to punishment or harsh discipline instantly might turn the clock back to loud, mouthy, tantruming days.

6.   **YOUR CHILD** plays salesman. Children persuade you to "lay off" the strategy–stuff for a while because they will do good behavior on their own, without your help. But, whoops! Guess what happens within a week or two. Remember those dark, gloomy days and long nights kept awake with headaches? Well, "hello again."

7.   **YOUR CHILD** hates you for being so strict with the therapist's regimen. You feel guilty and lay off the methods hoping to restore good tidings with your child. It works, for a day or two.

Is behavior change consistent with your purpose for therapy? Improvement is exciting and really gets the juices flowing. Everyone—therapist, you, your child—can't wait to spread the fantastic news. Stop the presses; hold the front page—it's headline news! Except what you have to say has nothing to do with why you sought therapy in the first place. You sought therapy for one problem— say, to eliminate lying. Is the good news that your child now tells the truth? If so, dandy. If not, why bargain for anything less than what you need? Lying is why you needed professional help. And lying will continue until there are direct changes upon behavior. The fact that your child finally accepts the grief over his dead turtle means he has insight. But insight doesn't eliminate lying. Telling the truth does. So, ask yourself if great improvement is really the improvement you're looking for.

Does behavior change appear in many different places, not just at home? One of the barometers of real improvement is whether your child can do the appropriate behavior in many different settings outside of home. At school, department stores, restaurants, friends' homes, in the morning, afternoon and evening in different places. Behavior that transfers *from one situation to another situation is stronger, longer lasting, and really part of your child's personality.*

When Is It Time to Stop Therapy?

When you believe therapy works, does that mean it's time to quit therapy? At first it's hard to think that way. Every week for 6 or 8 months, even a year, you have received constructive feedback on becoming the best parent in the world. Can you lose that precious feedback? Is it worth it?

Yes, it is. Therapy has one main purpose. That is to provide you with clear and specific skills you lack on being more functional in the world. If functional means being a happier, more competent parent, then reaching that point means therapy has met its objective. Don't prolong therapy out of fear, anxiety or for the following reasons:

1.   When therapy dominates your life and nothing else seems important.

2.   The therapist keeps finding new reasons for you to stay, although the original problems were solved long ago.

3.   Your therapist has been unable to help you cope with the problem that you brought you there.

4.   You depend on the therapist as a friend and find yourself obsessively requiring the therapist's input on all your behavior.

None of these reasons justify ongoing therapy if the main problem is already solved. Consider the analogy to physicians. After your flu virus goes away, would you keep returning to your physician just to "shoot the breeze?" Probably not. And therapy is exactly the same way. Seek therapy and a therapist to evaluate problem behavior, to obtain structured steps on curing problem behavior, and say goodbye to therapists when the cure works. Your therapist will respect your decision and be proud of your independence.

Separating from therapy is a terrifying experience only when you let yourself depend too deeply on the authority or technical assistance of therapists. One way to avoid these painful farewells is making your independence another component of therapy. Call it the *maintenance steps*. Maintenance steps are guided lessons on preparing you for being on your own and taking care of obstacles, including relapses. Steps teach how to troubleshoot complications, how to keep your cool under unexpected pressure, and when the time is right for re–contacting the therapist.

Maintenance steps are your safeguard against feeling abandoned. It's like getting a warranty. You buy a tire and the warranty says it's good for so many years. You buy a house and the builder's warranty says call if there are any problems. In therapy, the warranty reads differently: *you do what you now know is the best approach. It will work as long as you do the stuff you learned. But you have a lifetime warranty. Call at any time if you run into problems again. But only call if you can't solve the problem yourself. Because you also have the tools to do that.*

Therapists who believe treatment is like education support this viewpoint. They are always there to assist you, to give you refresher sessions and even to hold your hand through another storm. But no matter how frequently you return, the goal will always be to send you out on your own.

You'll be thankful for that. And so will your children. They'll get to spend a fabulous lifetime benefiting from your strength and wisdom. And take my word—they'll love every minute of it.